TALK BACK

SHONTESHA PRICE

ISBN: 978-1-7353128-0-4

ISBN-13: 978-1-7353128-1-1

TABLE OF CONTENTS

ACKNOWLEDGMENTS

I would like to give a big thank you to the Holy Spirit. As I wrote this book He pulled me out of my comfort zone and patiently encouraged me along the way. There were so many times when I wanted to quit, but I couldn't because I wanted to be obedient to my Father. As I began to write I found it rather easy to talk about someone I love so much.

Cover Design by Mithun Miah

Editor: Ken Darrow, M.A.

Dr. Michele Neal- Sherwood/How Fear Causes Sickness and Disease, https://fmidr.com/fear-causes-sickness

How is life treating you? Are you living or existing? Have you ever asked someone how they were doing and they said, "I'm here"? These are the people who are existing. They have sunk under the covers and only come up for air. Life has thrown them a few curve balls and they've allowed their circumstances to suck all the life out of them. You know what I'm talking about. The people I'm talking about are a grump on a log with no joy; they never smile and they're always complaining, sick, down and defeated. They live every day to make it to the next one. I ask you today; is that you?

God did not create you to just exist, to be a number among the billions of people who are here on the earth only to get by barely making it. Well, Christians aren't supposed to be barely making it or just getting by. Neither should they dread getting up in the morning. We're supposed to be LIVING, active, thriving, vigorous and strong.

God's plan for us is to live an abundant life with zeal and purpose, a life of power and authority with so many victories you can write a book. You are created to be like Jesus. We are made in His image to look like Him, talk like Him and act like Him. Our duty is to tell the good news, heal the sick, raise the dead and set people free from demonic spirits.

In this book I am going to tell you how God healed me of 23 different symptoms/ conditions in my body. I hope to answer many of your questions as well as show you how to live a life of victory and divine health. I don't think people know that their heart and mouth need to be saying the same thing. If you believe in your heart you can tell by the words that come out of your mouth. Faith has a certain sound. Faith speaks. You will no longer be silent while the enemy is speaking lies. You have to shut him up and whip him with the Word. Closed lips won't get you healed. Now it's time for you to Talk Back!

CHAPTER 1

Relationship With The Father- Dig into the Details

If you go to Facebook or any social media site, you will see tons of people. You will see lots of pictures and videos of life events with the children, husband and wife, date nights, family vacations, dance recitals, basketball games and more. You'll see the joy of a new baby being born or the sorrow of a family losing a loved one. You will see some type of relationship being shown on these sites.

The Bible from Genesis to Revelation is one big love story. It is about the relationship between God and man. Relationships are about being connected with someone, getting to know them, communicating with them, and having a deep understanding of who that person is. Knowing their character and detailed information about that person is also important. How well you know a person determines whether or not you can trust them. That's all faith is, absolute trust in God. Being sold out that He will do what He said.

So I thought about when my husband and I first met. While having a conversation with him I learned that he didn't eat chicken. What? I had never met anyone who didn't eat chicken. Seriously, I hadn't. Especially a black man. I'm not stereotyping, I'm being honest. So I asked him why. He said that his family raised chickens and one day he saw one killed and witnessed all the blood from it and it messed him up. From that day he never wanted to eat chicken again. I thought that was so weird.

Here I am, years later, and I'm thinking about what else would have unfolded if I had kept asking questions and dug a little deeper. I know I would've learned more about him and gotten a deeper understanding of who he is from one simple conversation about chicken.

Relationships grow by the people involved knowing detailed information about one another. I think the biggest lie that has ever been told is that we can't question God. What relationship do you know of where you don't ask each other questions? People are taught that by questioning God you are in unbelief or disrespecting Him. Oh, and that's a no-no! I was told you better not go there. I'm saying to you ask Him questions; He doesn't mind.

I think one of the awesome things about our relationship with God is that you can ask Him anything. Whatever you want to know He'll tell you. God welcomes your questions (James 1:5–6).

Always consider your motives. You need to ask with pure motives. Make sure when you question God it's because you sincerely or desperately need a right answer about a particular thing. You always want to do what's right. Your desire should be to understand Him and the Word better so you won't be deceived. It's good to have a better understanding for every area of your life. Who better to talk to about it than God? God questions us as a way to show us ourselves and draw us close to Him. It also opens our mind up to think more deeply.

Look at Adam and Eve in the garden. God asked them, "Who told you that you were naked?" Then He asked Jonah why he was angry. How about the woman at the well? I use this approach in many situations. Instead of making statements, ask a question about it. You get awesome results.

I grew up in my house as an only child for many years. I talked a lot and asked a whole lot of questions. What child do you know who doesn't?

Matthew 18:3 says, And He says, "Truly I tell you unless you change and become like little children, you will never enter the kingdom of heaven."

A child doesn't depend on themselves very much. They trust their parents fully to take care of them. They don't mind saying what's on their minds and can express it well. That's the type of relationship our God wanted with us from the beginning of creation, one where we know Him as a Father who longs for us to know His love and we are children who constantly need it and will never be without it (Romans 8:37–39). We have to draw close to Him in total trust and dependence.

Oh, to enjoy His presence every second of the day. His love always being there and never slacking. Never! He wanted us to be His people and He be our God. A people who needed to be cared for and a God who supplies every need. We are always on His mind. He promised never to leave or abandon us.

God wanted a forever family to spend all eternity with. Forever family is a term that Social Services use when foster children get adopted. They no longer have to go from family to family. The Father/child relationship we have with God helps us to trust Him. That's why I feel a need to explain this. Let me ask you this. Would your earthly father hand you a cup full of poison to drink knowing it could kill you? No! Not a father in his right mind. Well, neither would our Heavenly Father give us cancer or heart disease. He would never give that to us or any other sickness. He loves us too much to do something so cruel to us. God said He'll never be angry with us again. This is what we have as a covenant, people. s satanic bondage and we are free from that today and every day.

The Two Covenants - A Love Story

I want you to understand the difference between the two covenants and also know how God sees sin. I say this because understanding these two will determine what kind of relationship you will have with God. I was a born-again believer in Jesus Christ but living under both covenants, all mixed up. In order to live in divine health, you have to know how much God loves you. It all boils down to having knowledge of God's love for you and understanding the new covenant. This is how faith works, by love. Hang in there because it's setting you up to receive what belongs to you and always has. Divine health!

I was in bondage and didn't even know it until the truth made me free. The more truth you know about God the deeper your love for Him will grow and the more your faith grows. As your faith grows you learn who you are and increase the power and authority you operate in. You have to renew your mind to how much God loves you. That's where the victory is at.

When God created Adam and Eve, He gave them dominion over the earth and told them to subdue it. The definition of dominion according to dictionary.com means to govern; control; rule; subdue means to: bring under subjection; to overcome. He wanted them to manage the earth, keep everything under control and enjoy its pleasures. All creatures were to submit to them. They ruled the world. When man sinned in the garden by eating the forbidden fruit, they (Adam and Eve) gave up their authority to rule the earth and gave it to Satan. Their disobedience to God caused sin to enter into the earth and the earth became cursed. The moment they sinned they died spiritually. It blocked them from being able to know God on a personal level like parent and child.

We are made of three parts; Spirit, Soul and Body. The spirit is that part of us that can respond to God and have a relationship with Him. It's the life in us. No spirit, no life. The soul is our mind, will, intellect and seat of our emotions. The body is what houses it all. It's a covering, the physical aspect of us. So you are a spirit that has a soul and lives in a body.

When man sinned, they were spiritually separated from God. This was when their hearts became hardened towards God. Sin is what caused this hardened heart. Now every human being born after Adam and Eve is born with this sin nature, meaning they're born with the capacity and urge to sin. You naturally want to do bad and can't help yourself to stop it even if you want to. When a baby is born, they don't have to learn to act badly; they can lie by the time they're two. Instead they have to be taught how to be good and how to tell the truth. That's because we are born with a sin nature, an urge to sin.

The more I sit here and think deeply on the Word, especially Genesis, I'm right there living out the scriptures in my imagination. Bear with me if you will. I can hear God saying, "They just didn't trust me." It displeased God that they didn't think He could take care of them. I can feel God's heart and hear Him saying, "I wasn't enough." Many people know God loves them. But have they ever considered how much He wants to be loved back? We are made in His image and likeness. We yearn to be loved. Where do you think we got that from? From God. He wants to be loved too.

In the beginning, man was never meant to die. God created us to live forever.

In Genesis 3:17 He said to Adam, "Because you listened to your wife and ate from the tree about which I commanded you, 'You must not eat from it,' cursed is the ground because of you; through painful toil you will eat food from it all the days of your life."

Adam and Eve's sin caused them to die spiritually and changed the functioning of the heart. Now the heart was inclined to disobey God. Every person born has inherited that same heart.

As people multiplied in the earth man became more evil and hardened towards God. A hardened heart focuses on everything that satisfies your physical senses, so much to the point where you can't hear from God or see His goodness in your life. That's where Adam and Eve messed up. The earth was for their pleasure, a big ole playground. And every toy imaginable was there for them to play with. And anything else they wanted all they had to do was ask for it.

Satan's job is to make a garbage dumpster full of trash look more enticing than a treasure chest full of gold. He shines it up on the outside and waxes it down to make it appear valuable. It looks like the real deal, but once you open it up and look inside you realize it's trash. You've been duped and it stinks real bad. Looks are so deceiving. He's nothing but a copycat and a fake! God always has the real deal, the original—the original that has all the value.

Eve was focused on that one tree that she could not have. Her physical sense caused her to take her eyes off God. She saw it, touched it, probably smelled and therefore had to taste it. She became carnal. A carnal mind is an enemy towards God. It's rooted in selfishness. That one sin changed the whole world. It caused man's heart to become unyielding, cruel, impenetrable, uncaring, resistant and unable to relate to God. One sin ruined the very thing we were created for, to be able to connect with God. Man looks at the outward appearance, but God looks at the heart (1 Samuel 16:7).

God sees things about us that no one else knows. He can see straight through a wall, cement, brick, metal and rock. He knows every particle that it is made of. Anything that has ever been on this earth was made from something He created. He knows the number of hairs on a person's head. He can see through mountains and all the way down beneath the earth into the deepest pit (Revelation 9:12; Philippians 2:1). Surely He can see into man's heart and know his ways (1Kings 8:39).

The heart is the real issue. It's unable to relate to God. It became so bad that the whole human race was contaminated and corrupt. So God destroyed the whole human race except one man named Noah, who was righteous, and his family, eight of them in all. Okay, now we have a fresh batch of people. Instead of starting with two we got eight.

Can you imagine having a big house, car and a big yard with pretty green grass and no one to share it with (no family, no children, nothing, only a neighbor across the street that you bump into when you get the mail out the box, sometimes you may speak and chit chat for a few minutes then back in the house you go, no attachments)?

That's why God created the family with children so they could be connected to one another and experience a relationship symbolic of the one we have with Him and Christ with the church. That's what God wanted when he created us, a continual attachment, forever hooked up to Him, where He Is our God and we are His people, a people that recognize and acknowledge that they need Him continually.

Noah and his family repopulated the earth but inherited the same wicked heart and through them many nations were born. God still wanted a people He could call His own that would trust Him and worship Him only. Of all the nations of the earth God chose Israel. Israel was special to God because it was made up of Abraham's descendants. He was a man who believed in God's provisions and promises to him. He proved his faith in God by believing Him when he was told that he would have a son in his old age. God credited His confidence in the promise that He made to him as righteousness. God was so pleased that he made a covenant with Abraham that through Him all nations would be blessed.

The nation of Israel was founded from his descendants and this was carried out by God to fulfill his promise. He chose Abraham, who was righteous, hoping that he would teach his children, his children's children and generations to come to live God's way. God wanted a nation that would put Him first and worship Him. He wanted to take care of them and be a Father to them individually and as a nation.

Genesis 18:18–19 "Seeing that Abraham shall surely become a great and mighty nation, and all the nations of the earth shall be blessed in him?19 For I know him, that he will command his children and his household after him, and they shall keep the way of the Lord, to do justice and judgement; that the Lord may bring upon Abraham that which He had spoken of him: to do righteousness and justice, that the Lord may bring to Abraham what He has spoken to him."

Deuteronomy 7:6–8 For thou art an holy people unto the Lord thy God: the Lord hath chosen thee to be a special people unto himself, above all people that are upon the face of the earth

7. The Lord did not set his love upon you nor choose you, because ye were more in number than any people; for ye were the fewest of all people:8 But because the Lord loves you, and because he would keep the oath which he had sworn unto your fathers, hath the Lord brought you out with a mighty hand, and redeemed you out of the house of bondmen, from the hand of Pharaoh king of Egypt.

God loved Israel. They were His firstborn nation who made Him their God. They were His prized possession, one who was set apart from the rest of the nations on Earth to be a showpiece of His grace, glory and holiness. The more I read through Genesis and meditate on scriptures the more I see the heart of God. Can you see it? When you read, place yourself right there with the characters. Let God talk to you, become one of the descendants of Israel. Even imagine yourself being alongside Him, intimately paying attention to all the little details of what He sees and what He's saying. Look at His faithfulness to Abraham and how He cared for them and His power to fulfill every word that came out of His mouth. Can you see His love for them and

His deep desire to have a family that would love Him back?

People know that God loves them. They've heard of His love. How He loves us. I think people think He's obligated and supposed to because He's God. His love is not forced. He doesn't just love us, He is love. For too long we have trampled on His kindness and taken Him for granted. All He ever wanted was to have an intimate relationship with us and to be worshipped and glorified. He wants to be important to us. Okay, let me move on. I had a moment.

We're talking about Israel being His trophy piece (Exodus 19:5–8). Now, God gave them the law to create moral standards so they could see their sinfulness. The law was created to expose outwardly what was really in their hearts. It uncovered their rebellion towards God proving that they really didn't have faith in Him. They didn't trust that He could provide for them or protect them.

See God is still eyeballing the heart. He's checking out the motives and attitude of it, whether it's sincere or fake. The Bible tells us to put on Christ not put on. Man had no authority and no power but they did have God. All they had to do was put their confidence and total trust in Him for everything. All but a few failed at that. Loving God and one another had always been His plan. It's nothing new in the new covenant. That has been His plan for us since the beginning.

I have four children and two grandchildren. I can't even count how many times I've lectured my kids about them getting along and loving each other. I've repeatedly told them that they are family. Brothers and sisters don't fight; they love each other and have each other's back. Anybody with kids knows what I'm talking about. You've given the lecture too. Well, where do you think we got that from?

I believe God put that in us when He created us. It's His character coming out of us. This has always been from the beginning.

I have watched talk shows where there's a person usually around their 30s or older looking for their biological parents. All were adopted or never knew who either their mother or father was. I know it's not always the case, but the ones I've watched were raised very well, had parents that really loved them and were very supportive. They lived a decent life. They had to know their real parents and know if they had biological sisters and brothers. They wanted to know if they looked like them, if they were ever thought about and why they never tried to find them.

At first I wondered why they even cared. What I hadn't even realized was that I've experienced those same yearnings. The pain from it is real. The rejection and probably every other feeling they had I had too. I wasn't born again so I didn't know those feelings had names like rejection. It wasn't until it happened to someone very close to me and they went through it too that my own hurts were brought to light. A person can have the best adopted parents, foster parent or stepparents. Whatever word you want to put in the front of the word parents, they are still people who loved and raised you. Somehow still deep down inside something is missing. Why? Some were even raised from babies by others and didn't have any knowledge of their biological parent until they were told. So why search, especially if they had a good life?

I asked God and He explained it to me like this. When a mother and father come together, God chooses the sperm and egg. He chooses one each from the mother and father out of millions. Hand-picked by God, He chose to give that union a life, which begins at the moment of conception. God is the giver of that life. He knows us before we are in our mother's womb. Uniquely designed by God. Out of a million sperms we are specially chosen. That's big. See how special you are. Seriously. That man chose that woman and vice versa, but God chose the seed. He chose the child and gave parents the responsibility and privilege of taking care of him/her. The connection between the mother, father and child is a spiritual connection. The family was never meant to be separated. Children are created to have a lifelong relationship with their parents and siblings. To be connected with them forever. Even when they are married and have a family of their own the connection doesn't end. It continues to grow and multiply. The relationship is still there. It just grows. That's the way it's designed by God to be even though many don't have this foundation. So that child has a place in their heart that connects with that parent. If they are not in their life, they still have a desire to connect and relate because of our Creator.

The earthly family is a symbol of our spiritual family. Without God in our lives there's a void. You may not even know what it is that you're feeling. You could have much love in your life from family and friends. You could have every need met with many desires fulfilled. But there is still a desire for more. Something that's missing. I'm letting you know that it's Him. A relationship with our Father. I had someone ask me why their daughter, who was 18, was seeking to have a relationship with her father who throughout her life wanted nothing to do with her. Why is she so pressed about it and even care? I told her why. It's spiritual. She was created to identify with him in an earthly way the same way we are to relate and identify with God in a spiritual way. God put that there. Then she understood.

Psalm 139:16 Your eyes saw my unformed substance; in your book were written, every one of them, the days that were formed for me, when as yet there was none of them.

Jeremiah 1:5 "Before I formed you in the womb I knew you, and before you were born I consecrated you; I appointed you a prophet to the nations."

Galatians1:15 But when he who had set me apart before I was born, and who called me by his grace..."

Psalm139:16 For you formed my inward parts; you knitted me together in my mother's womb. I praise you, for I am fearfully and wonderfully made. Wonderful are your works; my soul knows it very well. My frame was not hidden from you, when I was being made in secret, intricately woven in the depths of the earth. Your eyes saw my unformed substance; in your book were written, every one of them, the days that were formed for me, when as yet there was none of

Now we have these laws—613 of them—that they had to memorize and obey. If they obeyed God and kept their end of the agreement they would receive all the blessings God promised them; if not, curses would fall on them.

Again, God wants their loyalty to Him and Him only. He wants to be their One and Only God who they love and follow, to care for them and they will experience His love and faithfulness. Deuteronomy 30:15–20 New International Version (NIV)

15 See, I set before you today life and prosperity, death and destruction. 16 For I command you today to love the

Lord your God, to walk in obedience to him, and to keep his commands, decrees and laws; then you will live and increase, and the Lord your God will bless you in the land you are entering to possess.

17 But if your heart turns away and you are not obedient, and if you are drawn away to bow down to other gods and worship them, 18 I declare to you this day that you will certainly be destroyed. You will not live long in the land you are crossing the Jordan to enter and possess.

19 This day I call the heavens and the earth as witnesses against you that I have set before you life and death, blessings and curses. Now choose life, so that you and your children may live 20 and that you may love the Lord your God, listen to his voice, and hold fast to him. For the Lord is your life, and he will give you many years in the land he swore to give to your fathers, Abraham, Isaac and Jacob.

God's showpiece, the nation of Israel, failed miserably time after time after time. A nation that was to be representative of His holiness could not get it right because their minds were on the law. Once you take your mind and focus off of God's goodness and love and lose focus of that, carnality sets in and one will try to satisfy himself physically and that's sin. All of your senses are engaged and you become a slave to it. You become controlled by what you see, touch, smell, hear and taste. It becomes more about you and satisfying you than pleasing God. Dependency on self leads to death. That's what the Israelites did. They were just as immoral as the other nations that worshipped other gods.

God was fed up with them and wanted to wipe out the whole nation of Israel. This was after He rescued them out of Egypt; they saw God's fury against Pharaoh with the ten plagues and the miracle of parting the Red Sea. Moses prayed and pleaded with God on their behalf. He asked God not to do it and God relented. One man's prayer changed God's heart and saved a whole nation.

God had a land flowing with milk and honey He wanted them to have, the best of the best. Come on, it had grapes so big they had to carry them on a pole. It was lush and super productive, unlike any other on the earth. Instead of being excited and thankful they were complaining and ungrateful. The sin nature is a beast. It's unable to respond positively to God's goodness and blessings.

What will God do about the condition of man's heart and a broken covenant? The one that has caused man to turn its back on God and His Holiness. By this time, the earth was full and all the nations worshipped man-made gods (gods they made by their own hands). Israel joined right along with them. They defiled the land God gave them by shedding blood and worshipping idols. So God kicked them out of the land He gave them and scattered them all over to live with the pagans (unbelievers). He punished them according to how foul they were living and it was foul. They really brought shame to the name of the Lord. These were supposed to be a holy people, blessed and prosperous, set apart from all the other nations; instead they became just like the rest of the world.

Everybody was talking about them and God. They made Him look bad because they were His representatives. The way they were living made it seem as if their fake gods were more powerful than He was. So God straight out told them that He was going to restore them because of His namesake. He had a promise to fulfill. If Israel kept going the way they were going they would get completely wiped out, killed off the face of the earth. God couldn't let that happen because it would make Him look bad. He had to protect His holy name. The mercy that God showed them was His choice. It had absolutely nothing to do with them. They did nothing to deserve it. Again, what will God do about the condition of man? The answer is found in a prophecy given by Ezekiel.

Ezekiel 36:26-27

26 A new heart also will I give you, and a new spirit will I put within you: and I will take away the stony heart out of your flesh, and I will give you a heart of flesh.

27 And I will put my spirit within you, and cause you to walk in my statutes, and ye shall keep my judgments, and do them.

This prophecy by Ezekiel spoke of a time when God would give Israel a complete makeover, spiritually and physically. There was no qualified man alive whom God could use to fix this. So God came up with a plan. There was a period between the Old Testament and New Testament where God did not speak to any prophet. He used prophets to speak to the people because no man could go to God themselves because of their sin. God's last words in the Old Testament were spoken by Malachi the prophet. After that, for 400 years no prophet heard from God. They call it the silent years. To them it may have been silent, but a lot was going on behind the scenes. God was making preparations for Jesus. Yes, our Lord and Savior was about to enter into the world to advance His Kingdom. God's desire for Israel to be His people and He be their God had never ceased. Every time I read it, it does something to me. I feel His love. The words jump off the pages and stay right where I am. His presence feels tangible, as if you could reach out and hug Him and rest in His arms. Read it for yourself.

Jeremiah 30:22 "You shall be My people, And I will be your God.'"

Jeremiah 31:1 "At that time," declares the LORD, "I will be the God of all the families of Israel, and they shall be My people."

Ezekiel 37:23 "They will no longer defile themselves with their idols, or with their detestable things, or with any of their transgressions; but I will deliver them from all their dwelling places in which they have sinned, and will cleanse them. And they will be My people, and I will be their God."

Hebrews 8:10 "FOR THIS IS THE COVENANT THAT I WILL MAKE WITH THE HOUSE OF ISRAEL AFTER THOSE DAYS," SAYS THE LORD: "I WILL PUT MY LAWS INTO THEIR MINDS, AND I WILL WRITE THEM ON THEIR HEARTS. AND I WILL BE THEIR GOD, AND THEY SHALL BE MY PEOPLE."

2 Corinthians 6:16 Or what agreement has the temple of God with idols? For we are the temple of the living God; just as God said, "I WILL DWELL IN THEM AND WALK AMONG THEM; AND I WILL BE THEIR GOD, AND THEY SHALL BE MY PEOPLE."

A New Heart

No human alive could remedy the issue with sin. So God decided He would redeem mankind. He would fix it once and for all. He would come and tear down that wall to make it possible to reunite us with Him again. He will have His forever family, sons and daughters that can never be taken away from Him.

While we were still sinners missing the mark and an enemy to God, He came to buy us back. Satan bought us with his craftiness, but God bought us with His love. He loved us so much that He sent His one and only Son to die for us as a sacrifice for our sins.

ROMANS 5:6–8(NIV) 6 You see, at just the right time, when we were still powerless, Christ died for the ungodly. 7 Very rarely will anyone die for a righteous person, though for a good person someone might possibly dare to die. 8 But God demonstrates his own love for us in this: While we were still sinners, Christ died for us.

The law provided a way for man to be right with God by a sacrificial system that involved the shedding of an animal's blood. This sacrifice was temporary and had to be done year after year. It couldn't address the defect of man's heart—the heart that produces sins. And those sins that earned us death. When Jesus died on the cross, He died for the sins of the whole world. All of the sins of the billions upon billions of people who live in this world were placed upon Jesus so we could receive forgiveness from God. One man, Adam, caused death upon mankind. Jesus is the one man who gave life back to man. Jesus was the only one that ever lived who lived perfectly before God. This qualified Him to offer himself up as a sacrifice. How? I'll tell you. If Jesus had committed even one sin, He would have been just as guilty as us. He'd be right in the same boat, needing a savior. One sin is too many for a perfect God. But Jesus was a perfect, sinless man who was able to offer a perfect sacrifice. And it pleased God.

Hebrews 10: 1-18(NLT)

The old system under the law of Moses was only a shadow, a dim preview of the good things to come, not the good things themselves. The sacrifices under that system were repeated again and again, year after year, but they were never able to provide perfect cleansing for those who came to worship. 2 If they could have provided perfect cleansing, the sacrifices would have stopped, for the worshipers would have been purified once for all time, and their feelings of guilt would have disappeared.

3 But instead, those sacrifices actually reminded them of their sins year after year. 4 For it is not possible for the blood of bulls and goats to take away sins. 5 That is why, when Christ came into the world, he said to God,

"You did not want animal sacrifices or sin offerings.

But you have given me a body to offer.

6 You were not pleased with burnt offerings

or other offerings for sin.

7 Then I said, 'Look, I have come to do your will, O God—

as is written about me in the Scriptures.'"

8 First, Christ said, "You did not want animal sacrifices for sin offerings or burnt offerings or other offerings for sin, nor were you pleased with them" (though they are required by the law of Moses). 9 Then he said, "Look, I have come to do your will." He cancels the first covenant in order to put the second into effect. 10 For God's will was for us to be made holy by the sacrifice of the body of Jesus Christ, once for all time.

11 Under the old covenant, the priest stands and ministers before the altar day after day, offering the same sacrifices again and again, which can never take away sins. 12 But

our High Priest offered himself to God as a single sacrifice for sins, good for all time. Then he sat down in the place of honor at God's right hand. 13 There he waits until his enemies are humbled and made a footstool under his feet. 14 For by that one offering he forever made perfect those who are being made holy.

15 And the Holy Spirit also testifies that this is so. For he says,

16 "This is the new covenant I will make

with my people on that day, says the Lord:

I will put my laws in their hearts,

and I will write them on their minds."

17 Then he says,

"I will never again remember

their sins and lawless deeds."

18 And when sins have been forgiven, there is no need to offer any more sacrifices.

So how does God see our sins now? HE REMEMBERS THEM NO MORE! Jesus paid the penalty that our sins deserve. God sees you now as He sees His Son Jesus. He's pleased with you because He's pleased with His Son. We shouldn't focus on something that God has forgotten. He's not angry with you. So you don't have to fear His wrath. He's our Father. He chastises willful disobedience out of love to draw us back to Him. He will never let us go. We are truly the apple of his eye.

God still hates sin and you should too, but He's not charging it to your account. He has forgiven sins past, present and any you'll commit in the future. So spend no time giving thought to it and trying to get it right. The Holy Spirit in you will move you to obey. You just have to cooperate. The less you focus on your sins, and more on His goodness, the less you will even want to sin. Now, we obey out of love and thankfulness, passion for truth and duty—a duty because now we're living from the inside out not the outside in. We are a witness to the world of who Jesus is.

Sin still has consequences though. Sin is to Satan what faith is to God. Living a willful sinful life pleases Satan and opens the door for him to steal, kill and destroy. That's the fruit of sin. God said faith pleases Him. The fruit of faith is an abundant life of God's blessings and promises fulfilled. So as believers we are to hate sin and whenever it's brought to the light in our lives we quickly repent, go boldly to the throne of grace and get mercy in our time of need, thank God, and line up with His will. Sin causes us to hide and run away from God like Adam and Eve. It makes it hard to appropriate the promises and block faith from coming. That's not what we or God want. The victory we experience on Earth is determined by how close we stay to God in His presence, not hiding from Him. Remember it's all about trust. How can we trust somebody that we're hiding from? Hate sin for this reason. It's all about the victory in our lives here on Earth.

Spiritually, we are already seated with Christ in Heaven. We can't lose our salvation if we're born again. God is not going to rip the new heart out and take His Spirit. In the same way you can't undo the birth of a child you can't undo being spiritually reborn. I spent many years living in fear of this very thing, which is bondage, because I really didn't understand this. Thanks be to God, the truth has made me free. Get busy renewing your mind. Learn of

Him. Ignorance is a silent killer. Oh, the love of God. Sometimes I sit here reading this love story and am in complete awe. I just hold my head and say, "Who wouldn't serve a God like this?" He's so sweet! So mindful, full of love and tender mercy. Gracious He is. My king and master! My friend! The great I Am!

Our sins have been forgiven. To receive this forgiveness we have to believe and put faith in all that Jesus has done for us, making Him Lord of our lives. The moment we believe in this, Ezekiel 36:26–27 happens. We become born again. There is a spiritual rebirth. God gives us a new heart and a new spirit. He yanks that heart of stone out of our flesh and gives us a heart of flesh. This is the answer to the heart issue. The old one has to be completely replaced by a new one. A heart of flesh is sensitive and able to respond to the grace of God. A new heart is tender and yielding, now able to experience His love, see His glory and be His habitation. God is now at home with us. The place He has always longed to be. His desire has always been to be permanently connected with and joined to us forever.

As a born-again believer we can communicate one on one with God. No more wall of separation; we are gifted the Holy Spirit, who enables us to obey. Obedience that's willing and joyful instead of grudging. We become a new race with a new Father, born of God, joint heirs with Christ, citizens of Heaven. Everything that Adam was before the fall. We've received it all back! Continuous fellowship and communion with God. That place in our heart that was designed by God that only He could fill has now been filled.

We have authority over Satan! We don't have to put up with anything he throws at us because we are filled with power! The God of the universe is dwelling inside of us.

Permanently living. Who is everything, knows all things, and is present everywhere. I get hyped just writing this. It sets me on fire! Salvation is soundness, preservation, health, wellness, prosperity, and deliverance. We don't accept sickness and disease, we resist it.

Sickness is demonic oppression. No, that doesn't mean every sickness is a demon, but I tell you what, he's behind it all. So I treat it as such. Even if we feel like his pinky toe touches our body in the form of any kind of symptom we put our finger up and say, "NO! Not my body!" The biggest thing about being regenerated, having this new heart and new spirit, is that we receive eternal life, not temporary life but eternal. With this we personally get to know God and our Lord Jesus Christ.

John 17:3 And this is life eternal, that they might know thee the only true God, and Jesus Christ, whom thou hast sent.

Jesus came so He could be what Israel failed to be. He was a light to the rest of the world and a demonstration of God's righteousness. He left us here to carry on, to be servants of our Lord and Savior by serving people. He died for our sins so we can be sons. Think deeply about that. We unify with the Holy Spirit as a team to continue and carry on Christ's mission.

This is what God wanted from the beginning, a relationship! With us! A genuine one that's not forced but chosen. He fixed the issue with the wickedness of man's heart and gave us the ability to love like Him. It's only possible through His spirit. This is the evidence that we belong to Him. The whole Godhead was involved and is still involved in our salvation. The Holy Spirit in us is waiting to become our best friend in such a way that we talk with Him constantly, Spending time with Him so He can reveal the heart of the Father and the Son to us. It's the Holy Spirit who gives us understanding of God's Word. The Bible would make no sense to us without Him in us. He is the power in us! Revelation tells us about our future and it ends so beautifully.

Revelation 21:7 Those who are victorious will inherit all this, and I will be their God and they will be my children.

I love you, Father...

Why would God go through all of this?

Pause right here. A question just came to my mind. No, a thought. Well, question. As I went to type in the word "plan" a few pages back I thought of how God knew all this was going to happen before He even created the earth and all of us. He knew man would fail Him, Lucifer would betray Him, and sin would separate us from Him. He knew how evil and wishy washy mankind would be towards him. Why would He create us if He knew how the world would be? He didn't just think of this plan. It already existed. Jesus knew He would have to die for us and everything. Why go through all the trouble of dealing with such evil being such a Holy God? I asked the Holy Spirit why. He told me that God was looking at the end rather than the beginning. Duhhh! That answer is so simple. Nothing deep but so sweet!

And I Love it!

Ecclesiastes 7:8 Better is the end of a thing than the beginning thereof: and the patient in spirit is better than the proud in spirit.

My dear sisters and brothers, don't allow the enemy's lies concerning your identity. Talk back! You are the apple of God's eye and nothing and no one can snatch you out of His hands nor separate you from His love. It's because of THIS love that you can believe in healing the same way you did for salvation. You and I were filthy rags when we got born again and we instantly became the Righteousness of God by faith. In the same way, believe right now that your sickness and pain was put on Jesus and instantly be healed the same way you were instantly born again. The same way He took our sins He took our sickness. Instant rebirth, instant healing. Talk Back Now and say, "I TAKE IT! Thank you, JESUS!"

The man behind the pen

Side note:

I wanted to go hard with the old vs. new, but this is how I understood it; these are the things that I saw. This is the direction the Holy Spirit took me in while I was writing this book. My focus, as you can see, is on the heart. God's heart and man's. This is what the whole Bible is about. Even when writing this book, I really struggled. God gave me so many pep talks and encouragement. I've repented a few times for procrastinating and at times feeling downright disobedient when I had pushed this on the back burner knowing that this was an assignment from God and not just some good idea of mine. God was serious and I had an "Oh well" attitude because I had started and restarted too many times to count. So I asked God for help many times. I knew I was making this harder than it really was.

Then 2 Peter 2:1 came to mind.

2 Peter 1:21

21 For the prophecy came not in old time by the will of man: but holy men of God spake as they were moved by the Holy Ghost.

Now I have the Holy Spirit in me, not upon me. Surely He will lead me in writing this book. That's when everything broke. *If He moved the men of old, surely He will do the same for me.* He told me to write from the heart. Then He showed me how the writers' personalities were not removed from them as they wrote. They had their own individual style and language. You just have to have a pure heart and right motives. Also He wants us to write out of a place of love for Him that's from the heart. Man that helped me a lot. Those were some of the ways that the Lord ministered to me while writing this book.

Talk Back!

CHAPTER 2

Get Fed Up!

The night had ended and we were winding it up with hugs and love before we left my aunt's fiftieth birthday celebration. We might have stayed a few minutes longer, but I started feeling a little dizzy. I wasn't feeling right so we left. To get home it was a 45-minute drive. When we finally got there, I could barely get out of the truck. My husband and son had to practically carry me in and up the stairs to my bedroom.

I knew something had happened to me. I was bent over and my body felt like it was all twisted up. I felt crippled. That's the best word I could use to describe it. I wasn't in any pain, just humped over and twisted up. I went to bed that night thinking, *I'll wake up and it'll be gone.* Well, that wasn't the case. I was praying for God to heal me all that day, but nothing happened. I remember going to the bank and the workers asking me what had happened. I didn't have a clue. I refused to go to the emergency room; I felt I was better off believing God.

That night, at home, I said, "That's it!" I stood on Isaiah 53:5, anointed myself with oil, and got in the shower. My shower is where it all goes down. I'm a superstar singing all of my favorites. It's my prayer closet and war room. It's my meeting place to talk with the Lord and where I get the best revelations. I began to sing praises to the Lord. Then my song turned to worship. "Lord, I just want to thank you; Lord, I just want to thank you; I wanna thank you for being so good to me, so good to me." Man, I got lost in that song. I forgot all about my condition and loved on Jesus. I must've spent nearly an hour in that shower. When I finally finished, I got out and walked straight to the sink and mirror to do my face regime. I looked up and all of a sudden I realized my body had straightened up. I was totally healed! I started yelling and jumping and praising God for what He had done. My family thought something was wrong. In tears I proclaimed, "Jesus healed me!" It was awesome. Not only is my shower all those other things, now it's also my healing room. No one laid hands on me, neither was I in church. There were no keyboard and drums. It was just me and Jesus. I faithed it and forgot. I forgot all about me and set my heart and mind on Him.

Worship invites God into your situation. You don't even have to ask; He just answers. It's His love. Love for God and realizing how much He loves you is the right atmosphere for a miracle. Also you have to pray. Not begging God, though, but commanding your body to be healed and settling it. Meaning that's it! It's done! Point blank, end of story. And it didn't even cross my mind again. I got lost in worship. Believe that you've received and forget about you! Put your thoughts and affections on God. Like that night, your healing will manifest without you even realizing it.

This was my second experience with healing but the beginning of my journey to divine health. From the time I was five years old until I was 38 I dealt with some form of sickness. I remember being really young and a kid made a comment about me having bad breath. As a teenager I had really bad stomach aches and I woke up feeling nauseated almost every morning. Also allergy and sinus problems were added to that. Do you see the list growing? By the time I was 38 I had 23 symptoms/conditions going on in my body. All sorts of digestive issues, gout, which is caused by inflammation, and female issues took turns visiting me. Not all at the same time every day but several of them would attack my body at once. I woke up one night with my big toe throbbing like someone was stabbing me in it. I think it was the worst pain I had ever encountered. It was so painful. I prayed and it wouldn't stop. I tried to beat my leg and shake it off like I would do when I had charley horses in my calves. The pain wouldn't go. Then I tried to swing my leg out the bed to go to the bathroom. Goodness gracious that made it hurt worse. So I couldn't get out of the bed. That night, my husband had to come and literally carry me with my leg stretched out so I could go and use the bathroom because I could not bend my leg. It was that bad. There was not a day when some form of sickness was going on in my body.

That night in 2015, preparing for bed, propping pillows behind my back, suffering from acid reflux with a dry cough, I decided that I had had it! This was it. This was not God's best for me and I wasn't going to put up with it anymore. I knew God was a healer and healing belonged to me. I had experienced it twice. I guess as long as I could function I tolerated all this. No more! I sat in bed that night and thought to myself that if something didn't change, I didn't know how long I would be here.

I woke up the next morning and went to the doctor. I knew what was wrong with me. It was a sinus infection and

I knew what antibiotics I wanted. The doctor was used to me coming for that. And he granted my request. But along with that prescription there were three others. I was familiar with two of them, but the last one I'd never seen. So I asked what it was for. Low and behold they were depression pills. I asked the doctor what for. He said to relax me. I was furious. How do you get depression pills for a sinus infection? I ripped that prescription up and stormed out of there. That put the icing on my fed-upness. I knew I was done with doctors. I felt so betrayed. I got home and prayed to the Lord. I must admit it was a little sassy. I told God, "I want YOU to show me what's wrong with me," like He was the reason why I wasn't healed. I prayed and believed God to show me what was wrong with me. This is the beginning of a wonderful journey of lessons, truths, discipline, revelation and wisdom from the precious Holy Spirit.

God will meet you where you are at. The first thing I did was search the internet and I came across lifestyle change and changing what you eat. One click led to another and I just studied my condition. I learned that my immune system was weak. From there I went on the candida diet and from there paleo. I saw excellent results within two weeks of no junk and straight organic food. I also took herbal supplements and used essential oils. I thought, *This is it! Everybody is going to be healed!* I was so excited to share my newly found secret to healing. I told my testimony everywhere I went. I felt that this was something hidden from people and I was going to be the one to tell it. All 23 symptoms/conditions were healed and went away.

I am a cosmetologist and salon owner. The majority of the people who come for service have multiple conditions going on with them also. So I started sharing my journey with them. I was directing them to some sort of way to eat or to herbal supplements. I was hungry to see people set free from sickness and disease. So then I became a health coach. God reminded me constantly not to turn this new lifestyle into a god. I remember Him telling me that He was the source of my healing and nothing else. He didn't want me to make the herbs, supplements and food into a god! He kept reminding me that He was my source for healing.

During that time I was doing so much googling and studying all the natural ways to heal the body through lifestyle change and all that stuff. I talked to God all the way through my journey. I didn't leave Him out. He has to be number one in everything. He said that He was the Lord our God who healeth thee (Exodus 15:26).

God wants us to trust Him, the Creator, not the created things. As I look back I see that my faith was in the created things instead of the power that was in me. You may say, "Well, God created the doctors, the food, especially everything that comes from the earth, and medicine to help us." Yes, He did, but we have to be careful about where our faith is at. In the words of Andrew Wommack, "Let's be glad that He made doctors because if not all the Christians would be dead." Yes, God created all of them, but man gave them power. A power that most put higher than God. How do we know? Because God is the last one most people go to for healing. When we've exhausted and tried everything else, then we run to Him when it should be the complete opposite.

God desires faith, absolute trust and dependence on Him. That's what pleases Him. Without faith it's impossible to please Him. See, as I told you before, it's about relationships. We don't put a coin in a slot machine trying to hit the jackpot to meet our needs. That's the way most Christians treat God, only go to Him for what He can give in return. If we pray a little, fast a little, read our Bible a little, ding, ding, ding, jackpot. God will give me what I want. No, He desires for us to intimately know Him. To Know Him the person. At the end of every, who, what, when, where and why you will always find a "Because I love you" answer from God. Yes, I was healed, but was it God's best? No, not by a long shot. Let me tell you why.

When you get your eyes off Jesus, you're setting yourself up for failure. Yes, I was still in my word and believed that this was the way God wanted to heal me. It worked because faith is faith. You get what you believe. I believed that God led me to all of this on the internet in order to teach me how to heal myself. Hey, faith without works is dead. It was all the work I was doing that drew me away from the intimacy that I was used to with God. You see the error that many make is self-dependency. We can't depend on self 'cause self will fail. Every time! Our Christian walk is all about total dependence on God. He wants us to know that He's big and mighty enough to take care of a cold, headache or cancer. The same God that made a highway in the middle of the Red Sea can take care of His own. He is more than enough. It pleases Him to take care of us. That's the Father that He is.

Think about it. Switch it up. When have you read in the Bible that someone healed themselves apart from Him? God said He does it and has done it. In the old covenant He wanted them to depend on Him for healing, and He healed. In the new covenant it's a done deal! Jesus has already paid for our healing. Look at the scriptures:

Exodus 15:26: If thou wilt diligently hearken to the voice of the Lord thy God, and wilt do that which is right in his sight, and wilt give ear to his commandments, and keep all his statutes, I will put none of these diseases upon thee, which I have brought upon the Egyptians: for I am the Lord that healeth thee.

Psalm 91:9–10, 14–16: Because thou hast made the Lord, which is my refuge, even the most High, thy habitation; there shall no evil befall thee, neither shall any plague come nigh thy dwelling. Because he hath set his love upon me, therefore will I deliver him: I will set him on high, because he hath known my name. He shall call upon me, and I will answer him: I will be with him in trouble; I will deliver him, and honour him. With long life will I satisfy him, and show him my salvation.

Isaiah 53:4–5: Surely he hath borne our griefs, and carried our sorrows: yet we did esteem him stricken, smitten of God, and afflicted. But he was wounded for our transgressions, he was bruised for our iniquities: the chastisement of our peace was upon him; and with his stripes we are healed.

Jeremiah 30:17: For I will restore health unto thee, and I will heal thee of thy wounds, saith the Lord.

Mark 9:23: Jesus said unto him, If thou canst believe, all things are possible to him that believeth.

Acts 10:38: How God anointed Jesus of Nazareth with the Holy Ghost and with power: who went about doing good, and healing all that were oppressed of the devil; for God was with him.

1 Peter 2:24: Who his own self bare our sins in his own body on the tree, that we, being dead to sins, should live

unto righteousness: by whose stripes ye were healed.

There is a passage of scripture where God had been faithful to this king for 35 years. God rebuked him for putting his trust in another army to fight with him instead of seeking God. God let him know that he wasn't pleased about that. Asa didn't humble himself to God's rebuke; instead, he got mad. Later, he gets sick and instead of seeking God He turns his back on Him and puts his faith in doctors. His heart had become hardened towards God and He ended up dying. He didn't have to die. God wanted him to call on Him and trust Him like he had done for 35 years where God answered and was faithful. (2 Chronicles chapters 14–16).

I'm not downing doctors because they've helped many people. What I'm saying is always seek God and invite Him into every circumstance you face and trust Him above everything. Let Him lead you and guide in the decisions about your health. You will get what you believe. If you believe you'll get better little by little every day then that's what you'll get. If you believe that the medicine will cure you then that's how you'll get healed. If you believe lifestyle change, diet, and herbs will cure you then that's what you will get. Whatever you believe and don't doubt, that you will have. Healing is healing. But if you trust in the power of all these things and not the power of Jesus' finished work on the cross, Danger! Danger! Danger! Focus! Get your eyes back on Jesus. If you spend more time seeking remedies and sitting in the doctor's office, meal prepping and ketoing and paleoing, searching for recipes and YouTubing, I can tell you that it's pulling you away from God's Word. There's nothing more important than keeping your relationship and intimacy with God hot! There's nothing like dwelling in the secret place of the most high God, resting in His presence. You may get your healing, but you will lack in other areas of your life. It will drain your time, money and energy. Please don't go drop your diet or change your lifestyle. This is not what I'm telling you to do. What I'm telling you is what I've experienced to help you to have the right perspective on our relationship with God and food and all the other stuff, to put it all in its proper place.

One night, I was in bed and my stomach started hurting really badly. Before it started, I was googling health stuff. The Holy Spirit was fed up with me and that internet. He said to me, "Get your eyes off that internet and look to Jesus!" Boy, that was sharp and, yes, I obeyed. I closed my laptop and lay there and meditated on the Word of God. I thought about how much God loved me and as my Father He would never want me to feel pain like I was feeling. As I was doing this the pain just melted away. See the internet can never do that. But there's power in knowing the goodness of our Father. Resting in His love for me healed me. Believing that He would never want me sick and by Jesus' stripes I'm already healed. Less than five minutes of thinking about God the Father and Jesus our Savior and being obedient to the Holy Spirit brought forth healing. I went soundly to sleep. That is the power of keeping our focus on Jesus. Our thoughts, our eyes, our entire being should be focused on Jesus.

This reminded me of the passage of scripture with Moses and the Israelites in the desert. They complained about being brought out of Egypt to die in the desert. All of this complaining came right after they had cried out to God to deliver them from the Canaanites who had captured some of them. God answered their plea and gave the

Canaanites over to them and they were destroyed. After this victory they forgot so quickly about the greatness of God and started bitterly complaining. As punishment for their unbelief and thoughtless murmuring, God sent venomous snakes along their path. The Israelites were bitten and many died. Once again they realized they had sinned by putting their faithless mouths against God. They went to Moses and he pleaded with God on their behalf. God instructed Moses to make a snake and put it on a pole. He obeyed by making one out of bronze. Anyone who was bitten by a snake looked upon the bronze snake and lived (Numbers 21:1–9). This was a shadow of what was to come through Jesus Christ. Jesus explains this in John 3:14–15.

John 3:14-15 King James Version (KJV) 14 And as Moses lifted up the serpent in the wilderness, even so must the Son of man be lifted up: 15 That whosoever believeth in him should not perish but have eternal life.

The Israelites had to obey God by looking at the snake in order to be healed. In the same way we have looked to Jesus and His finished work on the cross to remove the sting of death from our lives to receive eternal life. In eternity there is no sickness, pain or disease. None of that. It may sound so simple yet hard at the same time. It's not complicated though. That's why it's called the good news. Some think it's too simple to be true. Right now, just believe you're healed and act like it! Do what you couldn't do before. Look upon Jesus and be healed!

After my last encounter with the Holy Spirit I still hadn't quite got it yet, if you know what I mean. This last experience was a big notch in my faith during my journey. I received so many revelations on healing by getting little bites at a time. I was now a health coach! Yes, I went to school and got certified thinking I was going to change the world. What I'm saying is it's not God's best. Most people who go to school for years and years or have to do any type of extensive studying truly want to help people be well. I know I did. I sincerely wanted to help everybody. I desperately wanted to see people healed and disease-free, especially in the church. I knew God wasn't pleased at how many people who were born again were still suffering when His Son had died so all of us could be healed. It's part of the curse that resulted from Adam and Eve's sin and that curse was placed upon Jesus. I even taught a free health and wellness class and coached many because of my hunger to see people feel good. Not only that; out of the 133 cities in Virginia, Emporia, where I lived, was ranked #3 as the unhealthiest to live. There was and still is a passion within me to see God's people live in divine health.

Like I said earlier, I was healed and feeling good, but it came with a price. I took a three-hour drive just to go buy organic food. When my family went on vacation, we had to go out of the way to find places for me to eat. It was such an inconvenience for my family, but nobody ever complained. They were just happy for me. I spent a lot of money on food, supplements and oils. There were certain foods that I really liked that I dared not touch because I didn't want to wreck this new lifestyle I had obtained. According to my research from googling they would cause my health to revert. I had self-diagnosed myself with candida and that's a whole book in itself. Under this protocol I couldn't eat watermelon because of the sugars and this is my favorite fruit.

After three years of this I was kind of getting tired of this lifestyle. Tired of the time it took and tired of not being able to eat watermelon.

I started looking for ways to beat candida without the food protocol. I found an article on Pinterest. The title was HOW I BEAT CANDIDA WITHOUT A PROTOCOL. *Okay, this is it.* I was ready and excited to read it. She was a medical researcher who was studying candida. While studying it she ended up getting it herself. She stated that a lot of medical students get this and it's named after them, called medical students' disease. This is Wikipedia's description of what it is:

Medical students' disease (also known as second year syndrome or intern's syndrome) is a condition frequently reported in medical students, who perceive themselves to be experiencing the symptoms of a disease that they are studying. The condition is associated with the fear of contracting the disease in question.

This is why the Holy Spirit told me to get off of the internet and stop filling my head up with all that toxic information. You will think yourself sick. You'll end up worse than you already are. Words bring life or death. Whether spoken or written they're carrying something. Your mind will deceive you if you allow it. That's why every thought has to be brought unto subjection to the Word of God. All those articles that we read are words that do not bring life to us. You will not reap faith in your heart as a benefit from reading about sickness and disease and all the other stuff. It will cause more harm than good. The word of God is spirit and life. Whatever you sow, that you will reap into your spirit. I hope you understand this. Proverbs says this:

Proverbs 4:20–22 King James Version (KJV)20 My son, attend to my words; incline thine ear unto my sayings.21

Let them not depart from thine eyes; keep them in the midst of thine heart. 22 For they are life unto those that find them, and health to all their flesh.

The woman from the article went to the doctor and he put her on the candida diet, which we also call a protocol because it's a plan to carry out a treatment regimen. That treatment regimen is the diet. She followed it closely and didn't cheat at all. It is very strict. No processed food, alcohol or sugar of any kind and certain fruits and vegetables. It involves taking herbs and supplements.

She went to her doctor and got it checked twice and it hadn't healed after a year and a half. She was so frustrated and angry and decided that she was healed despite what the doctors said. She went home and got a big piece of brownie and a margarita and enjoyed it. She kept telling herself she was healed and she could eat what she wanted and she did. When her next doctor appointment came three months later and he tested her, it came back negative. She was completely healed from candida. She was happy yet totally baffled. She couldn't figure out how when she did everything right according to the protocol nothing changed but when she told herself she was healed and did the complete opposite of what she couldn't do she got healed.

I was waiting for this lady to acknowledge God, but none of that. She was an unbeliever. As a matter of fact, someone in the comment section had to tell her that what happened to her was called faith. She was so amazed she did a study on the brain and found out that our thoughts can change the whole physiology of the body.

Mark 11:24 King James Version (KJV) 24 Therefore I say unto you, What things soever ye desire, when ye pray, believe that ye receive them, and ye shall have them.

Can I seriously tell you how I felt? I was mad! Not that she was healed. I was so happy for her in that respect. I was mad at the fact that an unbeliever who doesn't know God or anything about faith got healed by faith. She stumbled right in the back door and got what belonged to me. Seriously, that's how I felt. Living by faith is my life. And here's someone who'd never even heard of it, didn't have a clue and got what I needed by FAITH. I was angry because I felt like she had what belonged to me. Here I was battling for my health and she just believed she was healed and got healed! I said, "No! Healing is the children's bread. Healing is mine!" Even though all the symptoms were gone and I felt 100% better, the slightest change in what I ate would cause the symptoms to come back! So here she goes and gets healed just like that, simply by believing and all those symptoms gone! She went and started doing what she was told she couldn't. *Hey, then I'm going to do the exact same thing and take my healing too.* I told my body to get itself together because today it was healed.

I was fed up! I went into my kitchen and grabbed the biggest bowl of watermelon I could find and plopped beside my husband on the couch and ate it. Then I went and got seconds, all the while talking to myself and my husband at the same time. Talking to my husband, I said, "Oh yeah, I'm healed, and I'm going to eat this watermelon and I am going to enjoy it. So she gets healed just like that and I've been on this diet thing for three years. Guess what, it ends today!" He looked at me not knowing what to say. He probably was thinking, *Okay, my wife has lost it. She's crazy!* He played it safe and said nothing. That day in my living room, I took my healing. No more candida diet, protocol, or any of that. No more symptoms, no more gluten this and that. I believed I was healed and as an act of faith I did what I couldn't do before. As if nothing was wrong with me. Just like that I was healed!

After all of this I went to the Lord and asked Him if I was wrong for how I was feeling when I got my healing. I got angry and I felt some jealousy. Like I said, I was angry and jealous that she was healed so simple. I felt like the faith she used belonged to me along with the healing that came from it. I mean that's how we're saved and that's how we live. Believers are supposed to believe, right? Faith is a lifestyle for the believer and a fruit of the Spirit. Here is somebody who doesn't know God, doesn't even know what faith is, but took her healing by faith. She showed me how easy it was to get healed. I think I was madder at that than anything because I had worked so hard to feel good as I was. *Here she goes and gets it at the snap of a finger.* I had to go to God on this one. I was jealous! This is the passage of scripture that was impressed upon me after I asked God this question.

Romans 11:11

11 I say, Have they stumbled that they should fall? God forbid: but rather through their fall salvation is come unto the Gentiles, for to provoke them to jealousy.

Salvation was offered first to the Jews and then to the Gentiles (Romans 1:16). However, they rejected it. Instead of receiving salvation by faith they tried to earn it by works. (Romans 9:32) By This it grieved Paul to the core. (Romans 9:2). So God made it available to the Gentiles. Even being born a Jew doesn't automatically save you. God has mercy on whoever He chooses. You still have to believe the gospel by faith. The Jews refused to believe but the

Gentiles did. Salvation belonged to the Jews, 4000 years coming and it was a journey. Finally! God loved the Jews so much He decided to come personally and save them so they could be a family that could never be separated from one another again. It was theirs for the taking but they spit on it and trampled over it and refused to accept it. This time, though, it was different. Jesus died for the whole world. Even the pagans who before would never have had the chance to belong to God now had that chance to know the God of Israel. It was the opportunity of a lifetime. Whoever believed in Jesus would not perish but have everlasting life.

This is what I was doing. I was trying to get healed by work. I was doing A,B,C to earn my healing by eating a certain way. I was the Jew and this woman was the Gentile. She simply believed that it was done and settled it. She was completely healed. No work. No protocol. No diet. Only faith.

Being provoked in this manner to be jealous can work out for your good. It's like being married. If I see someone flirting with my husband then I might get jealous. Not because the person is flirting but because it's with my husband. He is mine. He is bone of my bone and flesh of my flesh. I have a lifetime covenant with him. He's off-limits. She's trying to possibly take something that she has no rights to. She may not know he's taken, but I do.

God was jealous over Israel because they were supposed to be His people. They were in a monogamous relationship. They were His and He was their God. But they cheated on Him time and time again. They gave their affections to other gods instead of the God of Israel. The one who was with them from birth. This provoked Him to jealousy.

There's a big difference between coveting and jealousy. Coveting is when you strongly desire what belongs to someone else. It's lust. You gotta have it and it is a sin. Jealousy is when someone takes something that's rightfully yours or you hand over something that belongs to someone else. There is Godly jealousy and selfish jealousy. That's why I had to check myself to make surewasn't misplaced because jealousy is a sin. It's a monster and you don't want to get that in your heart. It will paralyze you and become a great hindrance in your spiritual growth. With all that said, that day I got indignant in my living room. I felt like I was provoked to a Godly jealousy and I took what belonged to me. I went back to Pinterest to find that article and it had been unsuccessful. I truly believe it was set up from God.

Testimony

In December of 2018 my family and I went on vacation to Florida. We keep our heat set at a certain temperature whether we are gone or not. This time wasn't any different. When we arrived home from vacation we found water on the floors of our house. Our hot water heater had malfunctioned and spurred water over on our broiler system and caused it to break down. Instead of giving heat through our radiators that's on the inside of our walls it shot out steam. This damaged large areas of our home.

We had to get a restoration company to come. They tore down walls and ceilings. My house is an older Victorian home built in 1938. I didn't think we should've been there while they were doing this but they kept saying it was ok because they had each area taped off with plastic and stuff as they worked on it. My husband didn't push the issue so I went with it.

That first night I slept in my bedroom I started getting sick. I was full of mucus and congested. I couldn't breathe through my nose at all. I was feeling so bad. I began praying and rebuking the symptoms and didn't stop. I noticed that when I went to my bedroom I felt way worse than in any other room in my house so I slept on the couch in my living room. Second night, same thing. Symptoms grew worse and it made me physically weak. The third night I tried once more to sleep in my king size bed but I couldn't take it. I looked over at my husband and let him know I was going to the couch. I dragged myself down there, frustrated, and tired. Tired of sleeping on my beautiful but uncomfortable couch, tired of not being able to sleep with my husband like a wife should, and tired of being sick.

As I sat on that couch I thought of Jehoshaphat in the second book of chronicles.

I had just finished studying this passage of scriptures. News came to Jehoshaphat that three armies had joined together to fight against him. He went to God and prayed. He boasted of God's power and might. He then proceeded to remind God of His faithfulness to Abraham of the covenant He had made with Him. He then went on praying, reminding himself that he was Abraham's descendant and a recipient of the promise God made to his forefathers. Proclaiming that God would fight for them as he did in the past. If they cried out to him, He would hear and save them. Jehoshaphat was saying how dare they offend the covenant that they had with God.

I was fed up! How dare satan offend the covenant I have with God. I'm supposed to be in my king sized bed, not the couch with my husband. Healing is included in the covenant I have with God. How dare you satan. You have no right!! I stood up in front of that chair and commanded him in the name of Jesus to TAKE IT BACK. Instantly I could feel my chest clearing up and going all the way up through my throat, then nasal passages and out my noses. I breathed a deep breath, it was clear. When I said take it back I felt all of the mucus, congestion, and all of that sickness being sucked up out of me. Satan did exactly what I commanded. He took those symptoms back. Every last one belonged to him, not me or God. I was healed instantly. Just like that. I stomped up stairs, slung those covers back on my bed and got in there. My husband asked me what happened. I told him that I was healed and that I will never allow satan to offend my covenant with God. I don't have to put up with him. He's defeated!!!

I'm stirred up writing this testimony. We have authority. You cannot tolerate nothing. You have to be fed up!! Take what's yours!

Do you see a common denominator y'all? All three times I got fed up and took my healing! Satan has no right to do anything to you. Has he stolen time from you? What about your loved ones' time taking care of you? Are you tired of doctor visits, money spent and relationships strained? You should be! A thief has invaded your life. Say, "No more! I will not be like this always! Today is my day; it's my time for healing."

When the enemy starts dropping lies on you in a thought, open up your mouth and TALK BACK. Tell him who you are! Here, I'll help you. Tell him this! Say it boldly. "I am the Righteousness of God. Everything that you stole from me is given back to me seven times. I'm receiving double for my shame. Joy for mourning and beauty for ashes. My latter days shall be better than the former. I'm not tolerating this anymore. I resist you forever. Flee from me! Healing is mine! It's the children's bread. The same spirit that raised Christ from the dead lives in me. Body, I speak to you right now. Be healed! Devil, get out my body. You will never occupy a place in my body again. I win! Always! In the name of Jesus."

CHAPTER 3
Faith It

Without faith it is impossible to please God! (Hebrews 11:6). It's a necessity in our relationship with God. It's something that you got to have in order to be a recipient of His promises. Faith is absolute trust that what God promises He will do. Guaranteed! This comes from relationship with our Father, spending time with Him and getting to know Him. That's something you have to make the effort to do. It has to come from a sincere heart.

When you get to know a person, you'll know whether you can trust them or not. If they tell you they're going to do something, do they keep their word? Do they lie to you? Do they bail out at the last minute and leave you hanging? People can have good intentions, but can you rely on them? You know what I'm talking about.

I have been in the beauty industry for 23 years as a licensed cosmetologist and salon owner. I can open my book and pencil in certain clients every other week for the entire year and trust them to be there or at least give me a call if anything changes. I've been asked to do that. There are certain ones I can trust to do this without messing my book up because for years they've been consistent and committed to this; therefore I trust them. They have never been a no-show. For at least 20 years they've been faithful to me, their stylist. Also they will not go to anyone else because they're loyal. I cannot say that for everyone. They are like family because of the time we spend together. I spend more time with them than some of my blood family. And I do believe it's mutual between us.

It's hard to trust a stranger. If someone came in and it was their first time as a client and they told me to pencil them in for a whole year and their second appointment was a no-show, I couldn't trust them to block out those appointments for a whole year and possibly cause me to lose money. They already proved that I can't trust them like that. The Bible is God's record of His faithfulness to us. It reveals His character and nature. He keeps His Word. He's trustworthy. We can always depend on Him, He never fails or disappoints. He's perfect.

We are imperfect human beings. Everyone has failed at something. One thing everyone has failed at one time or another is to love perfectly. That's why we can trust God. His love for us is never lacking and we can trust that He always wants the best for us, His children. Even though we are not perfect we can prove ourselves to be trustworthy. God places very high value on keeping our word. It's connected to faith. Why? You have to know the importance of it, and when you do, it helps you to have faith in God. It's about knowledge and believability.

I used to make appointments and I'm not happy to say that I was a no call, no show. I would say to someone when invited to an event like a wedding that if I didn't come I would get them something. I would commit to telephone pledges from charities and take months to send the donation in. I would fail miserably. Yes, I had good intentions. But I would overly commit myself or simply procrastinate and end up becoming a liar because I didn't keep my word. Don't let your words cause you to sin.

The Holy Spirit taught me better. The first thing He said to me was, "You will reap what you sow!" My business runs by appointments and we have to do unto others as we would have them do unto us. The reason why I felt like I was experiencing so many no-shows in my business is because I simply was getting back what I had sowed. Wow, what a lesson. That'll make you want to treat people right. Then, if i didn't make it to a wedding or baby shower I made sure I gave a gift. I kept my word. Even if I had to cash app them, I kept my word.

The Holy Spirit is our teacher. He teaches us God's ways. The point here is that our words are powerful. Everything that exists was created by His Word. While we're here our goal is to be like Christ. Our yeses have to be yes, and our nos have to be no! Keep your promise and your commitment because this shows the world what God is like. It's a witness to the world of God's love and character. It displays integrity. We are little gods running around here and we want people to say, "That's God's child over there. Look at 'em acting just like their Father." When you can see the importance of your own words and be committed to them, I believe you will see the greatness, trustworthiness and power of God's words to you. The more value you place on your own, the more value you will place on God's. Pray as you're reading this book and ask God to give you a revelation of His words. Talk to Him as you read. You will believe Him more and trust Him more and it will increase your faith.

Numbers 23:19 says, "God is not a man, that He should lie, nor a son of man, that He should repent. Has He said, and will He not do? Or has He spoken, and will He not make it good?"

If God said it, believe it. Then act and talk like you already got it! Thank and praise God for it!

God can only operate according to your faith. He could have healed me of all 23 of those symptoms/conditions that I had instantly. But my healing was progressive over time. The length of time and how I received it was up to me.

The woman with the issue of blood touched the hem of Jesus' garment and received her healing. Where did she hear that from? Who told her that by touching Jesus' clothes she would be healed? Jesus usually was the one doing the touching and laying on of hands. The Bible doesn't speak on it, but I believe her condition led her to determine the way she would receive her healing. We know that the only way to receive healing is by faith. It wasn't the garment that healed her; it was her faith in Jesus that healed her. Her condition had left her isolated and considered unclean. If she touched anyone they would be considered unclean. She knew the power that Jesus carried and considered that if she could just touch the hem of His garment then that would be enough to get her healed. So she did just that! She moved secretly behind Him and touched His garment. And she got healed! Be it according to her faith (Mathew 9:29).

I believe she sat in that house day after day bleeding, separated from her family, and eventually broke and got FED UP! She decided that it was time to take her healing. She realized she had life outside of the box she was living in. It was a by all means necessary type of thing. What did she have to lose? Her faith is now a testimony to the world.

God will meet you where your faith is at. I believed that if I changed my lifestyle and ate healthier I would be healed and I was. God would have healed me without doing all of that. But at the time I didn't have the faith for it. Some people are healed of cancer instantly by speaking to it, commanding it to go—and it goes! The person is healed. I've seen and read testimonies of people who got totally healed from cancer by praying over the chemo treatment. By faith they believed that it would not cause any harm or side effects and only do the body good and nothing bad. They didn't have the faith to believe God for healing without going through chemo, but they did have the faith that the chemo wouldn't cause any damage to existing cells or side effects. God met them where their faith was at. What I'm saying is start believing somewhere.

Trust God in the small things and allow your faith to grow and believe Big! With my journey, my faith went higher and higher as I grew in the knowledge of God our Father and Jesus Christ. I also was constantly renewing my mind and learning who I was. The new me! The more you know the more you grow.

You have to feed your spirit with spiritual things. You can use God's Word, teaching and sermons from Bible teachers, prayer and asking the Holy Spirit to lead and guide you into all truth. Guard your ears and eye gates as to what you look at, read and listen to. Many people minimize this and treat it as if it's not important, but this will determine whether you live a defeated or victorious life. Simple as that. It seems that in today's world people are not serious about winning. They talk a good game and sing many songs about it but are planting all kinds of rotten seeds. They're left wondering why they are faithless and immature. Their life is full of loss and destruction, just falling apart. It's because they are not guarding their heart.

Proverbs 4:20–23

20 My son, attend to my words; incline thine ear unto my sayings.

21 Let them not depart from thine eyes; keep them in the midst of thine heart.

22 For they are life unto those that find them, and health to all their flesh.

23 Keep thy heart with all diligence; for out of it are the issues of life.

To do that you have to keep out anything ungodly. In a fallen world you won't be able to do this perfectly. It won't be perfect until we get to Heaven. But you do have some control over it. Faith lives in the heart. And faith comes by hearing the Word of God, hearing it over and over and over.

So how do we guard our heart? We do it by being careful about what we watch, read, hear and think. People, places and things. You can't watch the game show network for eight hours a day and expect faith to grow in your heart. *Family Feud* can't produce faith in your heart. Neither can the Hallmark channel with all the meet-a-prince movies. It will not produce faith. Whenever I wasn't watching Christian TV these were next in line. But I felt myself becoming desensitized and becoming carnal. Things that I wouldn't usually tolerate became acceptable. I felt myself getting weaker spiritually. And I asked the Holy Spirit what was going on and He told me that whatever you entertain or are entertained by you will desire. I snacked on carnality and got a craving and desire for it. I knew that

I had to guard my heart 'cause out of it comes faith. And those shows cannot produce faith 'cause there's no life in it. I would spend hours at work listening to gospel music. The Holy Spirit taught me that all gospel music is not deserving of my ears. I have to listen closely to the lyrics to make sure they line up with the New Covenant. If not, it will produce wrong beliefs. Don't even sing them. Your words have power. Only sing what's true. They are producing life or death. Stop singing pity-party songs, especially the ones about you're tired, about to give up and can't make it no further. Romans 4:17 says. (KJV) As it is written, I have made thee a father of many nations,) before him whom he believed, even God, who quickeneth the dead, and calleth those things which are not as though they were.

See we have to call things forth. Say only what God says about us. When we do this, we do it in faith. It may sound completely crazy; don't mind that. Have you ever heard the saying that if you tell a lie long enough you yourself will start to believe it? Well, guess what; if you tell yourself the truth about yourself long enough.YOU WILL BELIEVE IT. Faith speaks! It has a sound. Faith will come. Whether it's faith in God and what's written in His Word or faith in the world. It matters what you listen to, what you see, what you read, where you go. Yes, I'm still talking about grace. This is not Shontesha's 10 commandments. This is what produces faith in your heart to live a victorious life. The just live by faith. We are faith people. We operate by faith. Faith in God is everything. I'm just showing you how it comes. It comes by hearing the Word of God.

Romans 10:17 King James Version (KJV)

17 So then faith cometh by hearing, and hearing by the

word of God.

Faith lives in the heart. That's why we have to be diligent and guard what we let into it.

Romans 8:6

6 For to be carnally minded is death; but to be spiritually minded is life and peace.

It is our responsibility to renew our mind. We cannot do it on a seesaw. We go to church on Sunday and Bible study on Wednesday to feed our spirit by hearing God's Word .That's about six hours or less a week. Then we go home and live the rest of the week and feed our spirit carnally. This adds up to about 112 hours a week (24 hours a day seven days a week, minus eight hours a day for sleep). Six hours the spirit; 112 hours the world. And we're expecting what from that? Not faith. The latter will win. Do you see what I'm saying? We will only get out of this what we put in. We have to hear more good news than we do bad news.

This is why many waver and are double-minded. They don't get enough of the Word so that faith can come alive in their hearts. Let's go hard for God! Not to earn favor. You can't earn it! It's a gift. But it takes faith to believe you have God's undeserved favor and receive it. Not requiring anything on your part except FAITH! I said all this to help you out. What will you be known for, being a carnal Christian or a man/woman of great faith?

Ephesians 2:8–9 King James Version (KJV).

8 For by grace are ye saved through faith; and that not of yourselves: it is the gift of God:

9 Not of works, lest any man should boast.

God revealed to me during my healing journey His best for us concerning healing and I want to share it with you. I had many questions. So I asked! I thought about the lifestyle change I had made that got good results but still had flaws. I ate organic food, meaning as close to the way God made it as possible, without chemicals, preservatives, pesticides, all that stuff. The problem with that was I had to drive three hours to get any type of organic food. Yes! An hour and a half drive one way. Then I had to shop and buy the food. So, yes, it took time, gas, money, patience all that, which was better than being sick in my body with 23 different things going on. And money was never an issue because my mindset was that it's God's will so it's His bill! I believed that God wanted me healthy so He had to pay for it. I believed Romans 12:1 and stood on this scripture for it. I was faithing it!

I asked myself if eating this way was how we are to stay healthy and live in divine health, then what about the people who couldn't take a three-hour drive to Whole Foods or what about the people who didn't have the money, transportation or faith for the money it took to buy the organic food? What about the people who lived in countries that couldn't provide this type of lifestyle? What if they only had not-so-healthy food and this was truly all they had? Then, God, you are being a respecter of persons because you're making something available to me and not others that you said is available to everyone. Healing is available to us all. We've given food a lot of power. We use it to determine how healthy or not we are. Most illnesses are attributed to the way we've been eating and what we've been putting in our bodies. Right. I just pondered on this for months. I just thought, *God, this is not fair. Something is missing. What is missing?* In the meantime, it came to my remembrance a testimony that I heard about a pioneer in the faith named John G. Lake. I heard his testimony several times from different people on Christian TV. The Holy Spirit reminded me of it, so I decided to order his book and read it for myself. He was a missionary in Africa during an outbreak of bubonic plague. It's a rare bacterial Infection spread by fleas. Humans can become contaminated by coming into contact with bodily fluids or tissue of the infected humans or animals. Many people were dying, but you couldn't pay anybody to touch the body for fear of being infected. So the dead corpses were left where they died. John G. Lake and a friend were missionaries over there at the time. They would go into people's houses and pull the dead bodies out and bury them, sometimes four to a grave. A large ship was sent over to Africa with supplies and doctors to help with the crisis. One of the doctors that came over asked Mr. Lake what kind of vaccine they had used to prevent them from catching the disease. John G. Lake had a revelation from the Holy Spirit of what it meant to be one with Christ.

1Corinthians 6:17

But he that is joined unto the Lord is one spirit.

John 14:20

In that day you will know that I am in my Father, and you in me, and I in you.

Romans 8:3 says, "For the law of the Spirit of life in Christ Jesus hath made me free from the law of sin and death."

Instead of the curse of sin and death being upon us, now we have life flowing through us. Because we are sealed together in Christ there's no part of our body that's not touched by the Holy Spirit. In Christ there's no sickness or disease, virus, bacteria or germ that can live because of the Spirit's power flowing through us and protecting us from anything that could harm us. To prove this, John G. Lake went and got a dead corpse and took some of the foam from the lungs of the dead person. This plague was very contagious. One of the ways it was transmitted was through bodily fluids. He took the foam filled with the deadly bacteria and put it on his hand. Then he told the doctors from the ship that had sent for him to look under the microscope to see what happened. When they looked, they saw that the bacteria died when placed on Mr. Lake's hand. Now that's faith! Now watch under a microscope as it touches my body, it will die and not enter into my body. John G Lake believed that He was no longer under the law of the spirit of death but now under the law of the spirit of life because of his born-again spirit being one with Christ.

Romans 8:11 "But if the Spirit of him that raised up Jesus from the dead dwell in you, he that raised up Christ from the dead shall also quicken your mortal bodies by his Spirit that dwelleth in you."

This is big! I pondered on this for months. I meditated, I chewed on it, spit it out, swallowed it and chewed some more. *What does this mean, God?* I kept asking Him for revelation. You can read a scripture and memorize it and quote it all day long, but until the Holy Spirit gives understanding of it and the light bulb comes on in your head, it's powerless in your life. Revelation moves you to action with boldness and there's no turning back.

You have an Aha moment when suddenly that scripture becomes alive in your heart. My Aha was that the life-giving power of the Holy Spirit, God Himself, was flowing through every part of my body. This glorious power creates a forceful shield against sickness and disease and nothing shall harm me! Anything deadly or harmful that touches my body dies upon contact like it did for John G. Lake. Bam! That's how Paul got bit by a poisonous viper and just shook the snake off of him as if nothing had happened. The Bible says he felt no harm (Acts 28:3–5).

Then the thought came to me. If no deadly thing can hurt them, then why are we so high strung on food causing illness? If a deadly bacteria and a poisonous snake bite can't kill us, how can food kill us? I had been putting all this dependency on food to keep me healthy. I was eating this way and that way, no gluten, lactose, this and that. How can preservatives and all the other stuff they claim will hurt my body kill me when a poisonous snake bite didn't kill Paul? He just shook it off. And a deadly bacterium couldn't harm John G. Lake! I know now Christ in us! Hallelujah! Christ in us! He's in us.

Revelation to a scripture or passage of scripture is more than just head knowledge; it's when the Holy Spirit takes God's Word and through His power reveals a truth and it pierces your entire being. It hits your head first to give you understanding. Then it penetrates the heart and causes faith to come. Next it hits your body and moves you to act on it! Oh, I'm excited! I kept meditating on this revelation. I kept repeating it over and over in my mind. I pictured myself eating what I wanted and nothing hurting me. I kept saying it over and over, telling people how we're one with Christ. I couldn't keep it to myself. Meditation is not only thinking on the Word of God, it involves images,murmuring and announcing this truth to others. You have to see yourself healed in this way. Nothing harming you! Get inside the scene with Paul. Picture being there. Now murmur this truth to yourself over and over again. Meditation is murmuring also. Talking to yourself in a whisper.

Has someone you trusted ever stabbed you in the back? Has anyone ever broken your trust by revealing a secret that you told to them? You find out what they've done and you are just as shocked as you are hurt by their betrayal. If this has ever happened to you, have you caught yourself talking to yourself in a low whisper saying, "I can't believe they did that." And you can't stop saying it. Well, this is how you murmur, in complete awe of this truth. "Christ in us!" Start thinking about what He did for you and how He died for you and now His spirit is in us. The same spirit and power that raised Christ from the dead is now in you! Keep whispering it to yourself. This is key to meditation. Share the truth with others and murmur it to yourself in a low whisper.

Always remember never to disconnect from God. Never allow your relationship to get cold or lukewarm. Keep it hot! This is eternal life! The healing, blessings and all the other benefits are great, but it's nothing without relationship. God likes to be pursued. He likes to be sought after. He wants us to know Him like Moses, face to-face. That was the problem with the children of Israel. They couldn't trust Him because they only knew Him for His miracles; they didn't seek Him to really get to know Him personally. Seek to know His character and attributes. God likes dialogue, fellowship, talking, laughter, and the outpouring of your thoughts and feelings.

The most important part is hearkening. That's when He talks and we listen then obey with an action. It's not enough to just know His mighty acts. Many know of Him in this way. They know it's He that wakes them up, it's He that blocked the car accident and He that got them the job. But still they don't KNOW Him. They only know of Him for His blessings. Don't get caught up with the created things; immerse yourself in seeking Him. Please, please don't make that mistake. If that's where you're at now run boldly to the throne of grace and receive mercy from God. Repent. Acknowledge your faults and line back up with the Word of God. He still loves you; we fall off sometimes. Let it be a lesson to you. Learn from it. Don't beat yourself up. God is merciful towards us. Hey, get back on track and don't look back! Press forward. You can't change yesterday. Only what you do today will count. Today, believe the impossible!

Talk Back: Lord, you are so amazing! I thank you for your Holy Spirit. Thank you for such a gift. Thank you for being patient with me. You're so full of mercy and you've shown me so much. I love you for that. There's nothing more important to me than a relationship with you. I want to know you better and see you for who you are. Teach me and show me your ways. Please forgive me for losing focus and getting my eyes off of you and onto your substance. I'm realigning today. I have the faith of Jesus! I am a believer of the IMPOSSIBLE! Thank you for being my Father and a friend. I love you, in Jesus' name.

CHAPTER 4
God's Best

I'm now healed from "the 23". All kinds of symptoms and stuff going on in my body are gone! I'm glowing and growing in the Lord, healthy and full of energy. It feels good to feel good! I like living this kind of life, the BLESSED LIFE! I got a happy dance to go with it! I'm now a certified health coach and I want the whole world to be healthy. I have information that can help everybody! The word has gotten around about my healing and now I'm getting speaking engagements. There's only one problem. They want me to come and speak about my healing journey. They didn't specify exactly what they wanted me to talk about. I knew, though, that my subject was healing. With my new title as a certified health coach and my experience with lifestyle change, healthy food, herbs and supplements I suspected that's what they wanted to hear about.

During this time the Holy Spirit was teaching me God's ways. He showed me how important faith and relationship are and how they are partners. I didn't know exactly what to share at the conference so I asked the Holy Spirit to tell me what was God's best concerning healing and I would teach that. That's when He said to me, "I'll show you." I only had a week before the event, but what I learned in that week changed my life forever.

One of the privileges of owning my own salon is that I choose the atmosphere and set the standard. So daily we listen to worship music or Bible-based teachings from my favorite men and women in the faith. That day, I was listening to one of them, Audrey Mack, and the title was The Power of Speaking in Tongues. She went on to say that she had a friend who was a born-again tongue-speaking Christian and brain specialist named Dr. Carl Peterson. He researched what happens to the brain of a believer when they pray in tongues to see if there were physical benefits. He tested it and there were amazing discoveries of what happens to the brain while praying in our heavenly language. The brain releases two chemicals that are 100–200 times more powerful than morphine. They flow straight into our immune system giving it a 35–40% instant boost or more depending on how long you pray. Healing is also triggered in other areas of the body such as the autonomic system and pituitary and endocrine glands. What is also amazing is that these chemicals are released from a part of the brain that's only active while praying in tongues. When released, these chemicals produce healing in our bodies. Another thing is that the language centers of the brain and frontal lobes that control our thinking and our will are quiet. So the Holy Spirit is in total control apart from our own mind. This is the power that's in us being filled with the Holy Spirit. We have so much in us that's yet to be discovered. I'm so glad I learned of this jewel right here. The more you know the more you grow!

This wasn't the first time I'd heard this information. A friend of mine had mentioned it to me briefly while I was doing her hair in the salon. I meant to look it up and read more about it but I forgot. So this time it really got my attention. One more thing is that the language centers of the brain and the frontal lobes that control our thinking and our will are quiet. Even though the Bible is the only truth we need, this study does prove that the Holy Spirit is driving and we are just passengers as He prays through us. That's why it's the perfect prayer. It's none of us and all of Him. This is powerful.

I consider it a privilege to be in control of the atmosphere on the job. Everyone has the opportunity to listen to these teachings while they receive their service and they love it. They think it's strange if the Word is not on. Thank you, Jesus! Many people have gotten healed and prayed for. Others were led to the Lord and were saved. I love sharing the good news. It is salvation to those that hear it.

Now I'm at home and it's Sunday morning. I'm up and in my closet beginning my prayer, devotional and quiet time in the Lord. I noticed, when I got up, I felt full as if I had just eaten a meal. I thought to myself, *I probably need a good poop.* It was just a thought though. Even though I meant it. But still it was no biggie at that moment 'cause I was just getting myself together. Next I got settled and I began to pray in the Spirit. After about one minute of praying in tongues my stomach began to rumble as if in a growl but more intense. I mean it was talking! After a few seconds I had to stop and run to the bathroom and empty. I said to myself, "Wow, I feel better." Now I'm getting repositioned again and start back praying in the Spirit. It happens again! I had to stop and run to the bathroom to empty. Now I'm feeling like new money. I feel good! That uncomfortable fullness in my stomach was gone! It was then that I realized I hadn't had a regular bowel movement in a while. So I sat down and the Holy Spirit reminded me of what I had heard the day before about speaking in tongues. It released healing in my body. I experienced first-hand the physical power of speaking in tongues like I had never experienced before.

Everything I had just heard concerning this, I became a witness to its truth. Well, where does all this come from? Christ being in us! His spirit in us. It wouldn't have happened without Him. Salvation comes with the best benefit package ever known to man. Romans 8:11

11 But if the Spirit of him that raised up Jesus from the dead dwell in you, he that raised up Christ from the dead shall also quicken your mortal bodies by his Spirit that dwelleth in you

Romans 8:2

2 For the law of the spirit of life in Christ Jesus hath made me free from the law of sin and death.

My second encounter happened while I was at work in my salon. A sharp pain hit my stomach. I immediately knew what it was. It was gastritis, a condition that affects the stomach lining. To me it was worse than labor pains. It hit my stomach and went all the way through my private parts. The pain is so great it can knock you off your feet. This is one of the conditions that I had suffered from in the past and actually had to get an ambulance called for me. That day, my first reaction was to call my husband, which I did, and ask him to rush me from home one of my remedies that I knew worked. After I hung the phone up I said, "No!" and commanded the pain to get out of my body and the pain left. My Authority In Christ is one of the things I was learning and putting into action. Then I began to pray in the spirit. That built up my faith to keep my eyes on the promises of God and not the problem. I had and still have my mind made up that I wasn't going to take any of the 23 symptoms/conditions back. Not one! I reject them. Once God heals you, you have to refuse to go back to the way you used to be. That's what I did. This thing happened so quickly. The pain hit me quickly and it left quickly! It all happened in about one minute. In the past it would come back spontaneously but not this time. By the time my husband got there it was over. I told him he was too late. God had already healed me!

1John 4:4 You are of God, little children, and have overcome them, because He who is in you is greater than he who is in the world

Isaiah 58:8 Then your light shall break forth like the morning, Your healing shall spring forth speedily, And your righteousness shall go before you; The glory of the LORD shall be your rear guard.

Third encounter

I will say it again, all of these symptoms just popped up. They didn't even begin when I was an adult. I can remember being about five years old when it all started. I grew up in a large family. I was my mother's only child, but she had 11 siblings. She was the oldest girl and I was the first grandchild in the family. So I grew up very close to my uncles and aunts. Most people thought they were my sisters and brothers.

My youngest aunt was around 12 at the time. I was such a granddaddy's girl. I would crawl in his lap to go to sleep or as a way of escape when I was being mischievous. One morning, after I woke up, I ran into the living room where my aunt was and started playing and jumped in her lap. She didn't like that I was all up in her face. She made a comment that really changed my life. She told me to get my dragon out of her face and pushed me off. Well, I didn't know whether she was serious or joking. I didn't know whether I was offensive to her or not. It was surely possible. I had gotten straight up out the bed and hadn't brushed my teeth. Then I had the nerve to be all up in her face. That's where it all started. Even if my breath was a problem that morning, it was an easy fix. Brush my teeth, which I did. Something happened to me that day. I internalized it. It's crazy that I was only five. Satan got in my head like that at five years old.

My whole adult life I was always concerned about my breath. I feared being rejected and offensive to people. I also checked people's facial expressions. I believe the fear in me became a magnet and I had a Job 3:25 experience. The thing I feared most had come upon me. It began as a mental thing, but then it became real and I battled with this off and on my entire adult life. I went to my family doctor, dentist, ENT, and gastrointestinal specialist. None of them ever told me that I really had a problem. And therefore I never got an answer or remedy. I really believe that this is what triggered all the other illnesses over the years. So, even though I was healed of all the stuff I had going on in my body, I still felt insecure about this one. I self-diagnosed myself with good days and bad days. I knew that by Jesus' stripes I was healed, but I found it a struggle sometimes not to feel offensive to people.

The one thing I want you to know is that God is not surprised. He knows all things. Everything! Nothing is hidden from Him. He knows if you have faith and when you don't. He knows your struggles and shortcomings. He knows when you're real and when you're fake. He knows the hidden things in your heart whether good or bad.

Every thought is known even before you think it. Pray to our Father with pureness of heart. Just pour it out of you. Cry out to him. He's waiting for you to need Him. He loves being a Father to us. God knew that I struggled with my faith with this one thing. I had to really renew my mind. I knew the truth, but I was always testing myself to see if I was healed instead of knowing that I was, regardless of the circumstances. It messed with me. Then I kept looking at time and asking myself why that wasn't healed and everything else was healed.

During this time a hernia also came back that I'd had complications with in my past. It wasn't a worry to me, though, because I used my authority for it and it went. This time I felt I heard the Lord telling me to go get it checked. I actually was glad because this was an opportunity to ask the doctor about a solution about the breath issue also. In my heart this was what I wanted healed more than anything anyway and God knew that I was desperate for it. I was hoping the doctor would have a cure. It really wasn't even about the hernia. The hernia for me was an excuse to go see the doctor for something that I really didn't have the faith to believe God for. God knew all of this and that's why He told me to go. It was like He gave me permission because at the time I was fed up with doctors and I was trusting Him more than I ever had in my life. So I felt like I was kind of cheating on Him by going. When He told me to go, I felt better and I was good now because He okayed it. Have you ever felt like that?

So I went and got checked and I already knew what they were going to tell me about the hernia because it wasn't my first time going for that. It was one of the 23. I had actually laid my hand on it and was healed. However, it came back. I wasn't worried though. I used it as an excuse because I know when symptoms or illness try to come back I refuse to accept them. I make them go!

Next I popped the question about my breath and she said she had a solution. It was some medical grade mouthwash. Yes! I was so happy and hopeful. I went to get the prescription filled and it was four dollars with my insurance. I began using it and immediately I started seeing results. I had my ways of testing it to see if it was better and it was. I was excited. After about two weeks of using this I noticed that my teeth were turning brown. My teeth were turning brown! Side effects from the mouthwash. Then the Holy Spirit said to me, "Faith doesn't have side effects." On top of that He said, "And why would you want to pay for something that I've already paid in full?" The cost to get that prescription filled was four dollars with my insurance. I got my answer right there. I now knew what I would be teaching in the conference. Faith in God is His best. Using the power and authority given us, knowing who we are and resisting the enemy is key to victory. We need a revelation of what it means to be one in Spirit with Christ. My subject for the conference was Faith: It's, Quicker, Cheaper, and it's PERFECT.

Faith keeps you connected and in fellowship with God. Keep seeking Him and His ways to keep the relationship hot. This is where you want to be constantly. We've given medicine so much power to the point that it has caused people to throw intimacy with God right out the back door. When people approach me for healing and I start talking about how by Jesus' stripes we are healed and that He bore our sicknesses and I begin to speak the promises of God, it's like a foreign language to people. They let me finish and then they ask what's good to take for this and that. These are believers and unbelievers both. We have allowed the media and TV and doctors to put food on this throne that determines whether we live or die. If you eat this you'll live and if you eat this it's going to kill you. Have you ever thought about this? Where in the Bible was food given this type of power over our life? The world has given it power. It has become a god today. Anything that we put first over God in our life is an idol, meaning we allow it to control and dictate to us more than God. I'm not telling you to go eat a whole pig to prove that food is not your god. The Bible says it's not the object or thing that controls an individual, it's a demonic spirit attached to it.

When I was on my healing journey and I was working on my habits and all of that, my faith was not there yet, so do what I did. Keep seeking Him and trusting Him with where you're at. The more you see Him working in your life answering your prayers and being faithful to you, trust Him more and more. I melt like chocolate when He just whispers one word to me. Okay, let me reel it back in. Now I'm back to the conference! God said, "I'll show you," and He did. You can receive your healing in many ways. God's best is receiving it by faith. It's Quicker, Cheaper and Perfect. How much time has sickness taken out of your life trying to get healed? How many hours in the doctor's office? How many hours separated from your family? How many hours on the internet?

Satan is a taker of life; God is the giver of life.

Do you know that Satan doesn't care about us being born-again? He couldn't get our soul, but he is surely snuffing out years from many, many Christians lives. They are dying younger and younger, killing any potential to win souls for the kingdom and be a witness and testimony of God's goodness towards man on the earth. When you pray, believe that you received it the moment you pray. You got a problem, find the provision in God's Word and don't budge. Sell out all the way for it! Jesus has paid for our healing in full with NO SIDE EFFECTS! "Why is this best?" you ask. It's all about relationships. It pleases God to trust Him, to show Him that He's more than enough; He is the great I Am. It grows our love for Him and we get to experience His love in this way. A God who is a father, friend, husband, provider, healer, protector, comforter and everything else He is in your life. He's our everything! The great I Am. Everything we need Him to be in every circumstance. How great. One encounter with Him changes you forever. Faith trusts the Father wholeheartedly; it speaks the Word and thinks the Word. You have to see yourself healed in your heart. Picture it in your mind. Be like a kid with a big imagination. See yourself telling your testimony of how God did it. See yourself healing someone in the grocery store. See yourself writing a book about the power of God and helping others receive their healing. See yourself cooking again, playing with your children or grandkids. See yourself being pampered and enjoying your favorite hobby again. See yourself healed in your thoughts. Meditate on scriptures, chew it, and mutter it. Instead of David with the sword, picture the sword in your hand cutting the head off the devil, who has stolen from you. Think from a place of victory at all times. If you wander off, line it back up. Sometimes it may take putting your favorite worship song on to get your mind back on Christ. Cast down crazy lies and thoughts that don't say what the Word says. Cast them down immediately! Immediately! Do whatever it takes to keep your thoughts right. Be violent towards it and fight. When I say violent, I'm saying to be aggressive. You cannot afford to be in wonderland with your thoughts all over the place. Put them in check. Say no! Replace them with the truth of God's Word. There is a great reward for this. It will give you peace instead of panic and power instead of pity. Victory instead of defeat.

Phillipians 4:8

8 Finally, brethren, whatsoever things are true, whatsoever things are honest, whatsoever things are just, whatsoever things are pure, whatsoever things are lovely, whatsoever things are of good report; if there be any virtue, and if there be any praise, think on these things.

9 Those things, which ye have both learned, and received, and heard, and seen in me, do: and the God of peace shall be with you.

Talk back! You have to learn how to open up your mouth. If someone says something other than what you are believing, with love, say, "NOPE!" GOD said, 1Peter 2:24 that by His stripes I've already been healed. If I were healed I am healed! I don't care what it looks like! Satan is a thief of your thoughts Don't let him rob you of what you know God said about you!

See yourself already healed. Refuse to see yourself in a nursing home, someone caring for you or in a casket. What would you be doing if you weren't sick? Think on that!

Chapter 5

Power and Authority

If we are going to be victorious in our Christian life we have to understand power and authority. It's a big thing. Our authority in Christ is part of our identity. When we are born again, we get a new heart and a new spirit, Christ's Spirit in us. It is by His spirit that we get to use this authority. Dictionary.com defines authority as: the power to determine, adjudicate, or otherwise settle issues or disputes; jurisdiction; the right to control, command, or determine.

2. a power or right delegated or given; authorization:

3.a person or body of persons in whom authority is vested, as a governmental agency:

We are kingdom governmental agents who are given the right to enforce the Word of God and bring it to pass here on Earth. This world was once ruled by Satan and he had authority over mankind until Jesus took it back. Luke 10:19 Behold, I give unto you power to tread on serpents and scorpions, and over all the power of the enemy: and nothing shall by any means hurt you.

Luke 9:1-2

9 Then he called his twelve disciples together, and gave them power and authority over all devils, and to cure diseases.

2 And he sent them to preach the kingdom of God, and to heal the sick.

Matthew 10:1 And when he had called unto him his twelve

disciples, he gave them power against unclean spirits, to cast them out, and to heal all manner of sickness and all manner of disease.

We control how we feel, whether we are healthy or sick, rich or poor, victorious or defeated. Point blank. But there are times when we suffer misfortune because of someone else. Other than that, though, we are in control.

Sickness is illegal in the body of a believer. We have delegated authority to command it out of our bodies. Do you see above that authority means to command? That's why so many believers are not healed. They are begging God to do what He has told us to do. He's not going to do it. He said He has given YOU authority over snakes and scorpions and over all the power of the enemy. He's saying to drive out cancer like He did with the money changers. Your mouth is the whip. Tell cancer where to go. It doesn't have legal rights to occupy any part of your body. Your body belongs to God and the kingdom of God dwells in you. Satan has been kicked out of God's kingdom. So if he's there enforce the law! You are a police officer with a God-given badge over the kingdom of darkness to rule and reign in this earth. Satan may be stubborn or forget that he has lost his place, so you remind him. Command it out of your body! Sickness is satanic bondage and you are loosed from it today! Pull out your whip, which is the Word, and drive that pain out. Don't stop until it's gone! Remember you have delegated rights to Jesus' authority. Determine that you will not accept it and then settle it!

I want you to see what's in us and what we're working with. The Holy Spirit that's in us is equal to the Father and Jesus. He is God. He's not the least of the three persons of the Trinity. The glory that's in us is the same glory that will illuminate the whole earth. Our spirit is so full of light that it puts darkness to death. This is the same glory that man couldn't see with his eyes and live. The same glory lived in Jesus who became flesh. He is the very express image of God. We have God and 100% of His goodness dwelling inside of us. This is why we are supernatural. This is why Jesus said so as He was in the earth so are we. This is why we can command sickness to go and cast out demons. It's because we have God living in us and through us. Our words have the same power that He spoke. The problem is we have to believe that we have all this. It's called faith.

God has given us permission to operate in His power from within and its results are seen outwardly. We as believers have to release this power that's within us. Power is physical, mental and spiritual ability, strength, and capacity. An elephant can use its power to crush a car, that's physical strength. A bodybuilder lifts weights by having physical strength. Years ago, I worked with this person who wasn't the easiest to work with. At times she was quite difficult and I thought, *Man, I can't do this.* I asked the Lord many times to remove this person so I could work comfortably and keep the ambiance that I was used to. One day, while in prayer, the Lord answered me and said, "I'm going to perfect your love." That was one of my "melt me away" moments. One of my constant prayer requests of the Lord was asking Him to perfect my love towards people. So He basically told me, "I will show you how real love works, my kinda love." He began to show me the root of why this person was like they were. Instead of annoyance, compassion for this person filled my heart. I began to pray for this person and my heart changed towards them. I wanted the very best for them, I became patient toward them. So much happened in my heart with this one experience. That was the power of the Holy Spirit working in me to transform my thinking and purify my heart so I could see her and love her as Christ loves me. This is the scripture that just wrecked me when He brought it to me.

Matthew 5:46 If you love only those who love you, what reward is there for that? Even corrupt tax collectors do that much.

This dunamis power was also described in signs, miracles, healings and the mighty works of Jesus and the Apostles.

The word ability means: power or capacity to do or act physically, mentally, legally, morally, financially, etc.

competence in an activity or occupation because of one's skill, training, or other qualification:

the ability to sing well.

abilities, talents; special skills or aptitudes.

God gives us the ability, or I'd like to say "know how", to get wealth. He gives us inventions and ideas, talents and gifts. We are creative beings because we are made in the image of God. Every time I look at my screensaver on my computer I'm in awe of the beauty I see before me. The Creator of this beautiful earth lives in ME.

David and Goliath is a great example too. Goliath had physical power, but David had physical mental and spiritual power because of who was upon him. He had the dynamic power of Holy Spirit operating. He knew who he was and what he had. A teenager. It does not matter the age. Whether you're eight or 100 you get the same Holy Spirit. Young people don't get a junior Holy Spirit. They get 100% God.

Now, there's a big difference between power and authority. Power is ability; authority is legal right. A person driving a transfer truck has the power/force to run you over, but a police officer has the authority to hold up that badge and stop him in his tracks. Satan had no power or authority on this earth. Adam and Eve's sin handed it over to him. God told Adam to rule and reign over the earth. He had authority over the whole earth, but Satan bamboozled him out of it. He's a lying, conniving trickster. But over 2000 years ago, Jesus died on the cross and God raised Him up on the third day. He crushed Satan's head and snatched that power right back from him (Genesis 3:15). Jesus took the keys of death, fear and bondage from Satan. He totally disarmed him.

God gave all authority to Jesus and everything and every name submitted to Him. What He did for us He had to do it legally because God is a just God. He had to follow His own rules. Christ had to die and God raised Him up all for us.

Colossians 2:13–15

13 And you, being dead in your trespasses and the uncircumcision of your flesh, He has made alive together with Him, having forgiven you all trespasses, 14 having wiped out the [a]handwriting of requirements that was against us, which was contrary to us. And He has taken it out of the way, having nailed it to the cross. 15 Having disarmed principalities and powers, He made a public spectacle of them, triumphing over them in it.

So as Jesus was in the earth so are we. He told us when He left that we should do greater works. He ascended to Heaven and sat at the right hand of the Father. When He was here on Earth He healed the sick, cast out demons and raised the dead. Jesus has all power and authority over Satan and his demons. He is underneath His feet. Jesus told us that He saw Satan kicked out of Heaven like lightning. He has given us believers power and authority over all the powers of the enemy and NOTHING shall hurt us (Luke 10:19). Jesus handed his power and authority over to us to legally use it as if we were Him. He took our sins and gave us His righteousness. Our defeat for His victory, and our weakness for His power. He gave it to us. We didn't earn any of this. He gave us His something when he had NOTHING.

When we pray, we don't ask and beg God to heal us. We enforce our healing because we are now in the Blessing. Healing belongs to us. So we have to use our authority and enforce, take what belongs to us. Satan doesn't want believers to know what they got. He's hoping they stay ignorant and without knowledge of the truth. The only way now that Satan can harm us is through lies and deceit. And he is good at it. That's why it's so important to learn who you are and what you got in the Word of God. Put on the whole armor of God and hide the Word of God in your heart. Say only what God says. Do what Jesus did and tell Him it is written! You will only take authority over what you know you have rights to.

I'm better at explaining it to you by sharing my experiences with you. This is how the Holy Spirit taught me, through encounters. I haven't perfected it, I'm still learning, but I've gotten off the boat. By the end of this book many of you will be healed by using your authority over sickness and disease in your body. Okay, Let's get down to the nitty gritty.

My first experience with authority was about six years ago. It was one of the coldest winters I've ever experienced in my hometown. We had gotten a lot of snow and ice. As a business owner, whenever it snows I like to get my parking lot scraped and cleaned so we can work and it's safe for us and our clients. I noticed a man in a tractor scraping a couple of businesses across the street from me and it was clean. I was impressed. So I asked him if he would do mine after he finished with theirs. He agreed and I paid him. He said he would be there for a while so I just went home happy that we would be able to work the next day. I did pay him good money to do the job, so later that evening, I went back to check it out. All the snow had been shoveled to one side of my building, but there was still this thick sheet of ice on my whole parking lot. I was not satisfied because the lots across the street were done way better than mine. So I went home disappointed. I had given my coworker an okay to work, so we had clients coming. I didn't want to have to cancel them and I wanted my coworkers to make money. I was more concerned about them than myself. I went home with it deeply on my mind. I woke up around 5:30 to go to the bathroom. With the parking lot still on my mind I knelt down at my stool and began to pray. Yes, toilet stool, and began to pray. It went something like this: "Father, I know you can do anything, will you let the sun shine so bright on my parking lot that it melts the ice so my parking lot will be clean for us to work tomorrow?"

This is what God said back to me:

"YOU tell the sun what to do!"

Me: "What?"

God: "YOU tell the sun what to do!!"

Me: "Okay Father." I stretched out my hand toward the sun, where I know it's at when I go to work in the morning, and said, "Sun, I command you to shine so bright on my parking lot that you melt all the ice so it will be clean and we can park on a clean parking lot."

Jesus did speak to the wind and waves and command, "Peace, be still."

Can I and tell you that I felt so silly praying that prayer. I had never spoken to the elements. But I prayed. God told me to command the sun! I was in awe and felt silly but still obeyed!

I went to work the next day and the parking lot was still full of ice. Everyone showed up. My coworker and our clients. I felt so bad because as a business owner it's my job to take care of this sort of thing. I told my coworker what had happened and she suggested that I call him back, especially considering the amount of money I paid him. I agreed to it but had left my cell phone at home, which had the guy's number in it. I left to go home to get my phone and make the call.

It would've only taken a minute because my house is right up the street. When I stopped at the stoplight, the Lord questioned me. He said, "Who are you going to trust, Me or him?"

I said, "You Lord."

I turned around and went back to work and didn't say another word to anyone. As my coworker's client left, about an hour later, she yelled, "Hey Shontesha, the guy came and cleaned the parking lot." I ran to the door and looked. Water was running from my parking lot along the side of the street as if it had rained. Mind you, it was way below freezing temperatures. Immediately I just started screaming and praising God. I yelled, "NO! My God did that! Thank you Jeeeeesus!" It was a miracle! I immediately thought of Joshua commanding the sun to stand still. That's when I realized what I had inside of me. The Holy Spirit wanted me to know. He directed me and taught me how. He trained me. Everything Jesus said and did we are to imitate. Since that day I have stopped tornados in their tracks and watched them die down right before my eyes. I've commanded the rain to be put on hold, winds to cease and hurricanes to bow at the name of Jesus and they did. Brothers and sisters, stop and meditate on this. You can give the sun orders and it will obey. Surely you tell sickness when and where to go.

I was at home washing dishes back in 2015 when I got some visitors. Their faithful came every year. The Ants family always came and raided my kitchen. My husband and I had used all kinds of sprays and solutions to get rid of them. Every year they found their way back. The Holy Spirit is so precious He brought Genesis 1:26–28 to my remembrance.

Genesis 1:26–28

26 And God said, Let us make man in our image, after our likeness: and let them have dominion over the fish of the sea, and over the fowl of the air, and over the cattle, and over all the earth, and over every creeping thing that creepeth upon the earth.

27 So God created man in his own image, in the image of God created he him; male and female created he them.

28 And God blessed them, and God said unto them, Be fruitful, and multiply, and replenish the earth, and subdue it: and have dominion over the fish of the sea, and over the fowl of the air, and over every living thing that moveth upon the earth.

Every born-again believer has this authority, even over the animals. I went outside my house and I commanded the ants! I said, "Look! God has given you all this dirt and earth as your natural habitat, this is where you live. This house is mine and I command you to get out and never return or you will die!" It has been five years and we have never had a problem with ants to this day. I cannot even remember seeing one ant inside my house.

Do you notice something in common every time? I got fed up! I was not going to tolerate it! I will say it again. As long as you're willing to put up with sickness, poverty, and defeat in any area of your life you will not see results. Authority is not passive. It's bold and aggressive. This is the same way you cast a demon out of a person or when a demonic spirit is oppressing you. God has given us dominion. The same that Adam had before the fall. God gave power and authority to man. So it's absolutely silly to beg God for something that He has given to us. Sickness and disease is from the curse of the law. Jesus took that curse upon Himself on the cross. He reversed everything Satan did. All of His suffering was to free us. Whenever any type of sickness attacks your body, it's doing it illegally. It doesn't have a right to be in your body because it was put on Jesus'. You are private property. You belong to God. Satan had his chance, but he blew it. Your citizenship is in Heaven. You are in this world but not of this world. If your home is Heaven and Satan got kicked out then he is trespassing. You have the authority like a police officer to command him to go, leave, get out, and get off that property. You are that property!

At our local post office have some pretty green grass by the front doors on both sides. They have a sign on that grass that says, “No trespassing!” That means no one is to put their feet on that grass. Don’t touch it! God loved us so much that He came as a man to redeem us. This comes with the benefit package of our redemption. These scriptures are so powerful. Take your time and meditate and think deeply on them.

Luke 10:19 "Behold, I have given you authority to tread on serpents and scorpions, and over all the power of the enemy, and nothing will injure you."

1 Corinthians 6:20 For you have been bought with a price: therefore glorify God in your body.

1Peter 1:18-19 (NASB)...knowing that you were not redeemed with perishable things like silver or gold from your futile way of life inherited from your forefathers, 19. but with precious blood, as of a lamb unblemished and spotless, the blood of Christ.

Matthew 28:18 (NASB)

And Jesus came up and spoke to them, saying, "All authority has been given to Me in heaven and on earth

Ephesians 1:20–21. God raised him from the dead and seated him at his right hand in the heavenly places, far above all rule and authority and power and dominion, and above every name that is named, not only in this age but also in the one to come.

1John 4:17 Herein is our love made perfect, that we may have boldness in the day of judgment: because as he is, so are we in this world.

Galatians 3:13. Christ has redeemed us from the curse of the law, having become a curse for us (for it is written, “Cursed is everyone who hangs on a tree”).

When Jesus healed the sick, he didn't say, "Father would you please heal so-and-so?" Neither did He pray, "If it be thy will, take this cancer away." First of all it IS His will to heal. When the leper asked, "If it be thy will, heal him," Jesus said, "I WILL."

Jesus only said and did what he saw His Father do. He was a representation of the Father in every aspect. God the Father is the one who gave Jesus all authority. It belonged to Jesus. Now that Jesus is no longer in the earth, He promised to send His spirit to dwell in us so that we can carry on where He left off. This time, instead of just one person as Jesus was, now there are millions of people with the same power and authority as Him. He gave it as a gift to us. When either praying for the sick or yourself, first resist the pain or sickness. Refuse to accept it and say, "How dare you attack my body? Satan, you liar! Jesus loves me too much. By His stripes I am healed! Go now! In Jesus, name."

Audrey Mack taught me that it is best to attack sickness at the first sign of its symptom. For instance, you know the first sign of a cold is usually an itchy throat. Well, as soon as you start to feel that itchiness say, "No! Itchiness, go now! In the name of Jesus! I will never get another cold again." Say it boldly and confidently. You are obeying God. He said, "Speak to that mountain and SAY. If you do not doubt, you will have what you SAY. If you say, "It's flu season. Every year around this time I get the flu," guess what; if you believe this, you will have what you SAY. You will have the flu. Simple as that. Only say what God says. You got to talk back.

The devil says, "You are about to catch a cold."

You say, "Liar! No! Back up off of me. You are trespassing! You have no legal rights to put a finger on me. Say what you mean and mean what you say. The fewer words the better.

Satan is full of pride. Prideful people love attention and so does he. The less attention you give him the more you will starve him and the quicker he will flee. That's part of resisting him. But when you do speak, let it be full of life and not death.

People will think you are being arrogant and crazy. They will say all types of things until they keep watching you and see results. Then they will start coming to you and ask you to pray for their healing. This authority that has been given to us has to be used by faith and it pleases God when we use it.

When I was growing up, my grandma had a bunch of what we call whatnots on her coffee table. Most people would tell her to remove them so that the children wouldn't break them. Not my grandma. Why? Because she had authority in her house and she had the power to stop anyone attempting to remove, play with or handle her whatnots. Nobody dared to touch them! Whenever someone got brave enough to touch them, usually it was the babies two years old and under, she would say, "Uuuuump!" or, "Noooooo!" Immediately they would snatch their hand back. I found out this works with Satan too. He is the root of all sickness and disease on the earth. While everything is not a demon, I treat it all the same because he's the owner of it. So when tinnitus attackes I just say, "No!" or, "Uuuuump!" And immediately it leaves. If I wake up and my eyes are running water and itchy I simply say, "Satan, get out of my eyes now!" I immediately command all the symptoms to leave. I realized it's all the same. Think about how you exercise authority in your job or with a child and use it in the same way.

Let's look at an example of what Jesus calls great faith.

Matthew 8:5–13

5 And when Jesus was entered into Capernaum, there came
unto him a centurion, beseeching him,

6 And saying, Lord, my servant lieth at home sick of the
palsy, grievously tormented.

7 And Jesus saith unto him, I will come and heal him.

8 The centurion answered and said, Lord, I am not worthy
that thou shouldest come under my roof: but speak the
word only, and my servant shall be healed.

9 For I am a man under authority, having soldiers under
me: and I say to this man, Go, and he goeth; and to another,
Come, and he cometh; and to my servant, Do this, and he
doeth it.

10 When Jesus heard it, he marvelled, and said to them that
followed, Verily I say unto you, I have not found so great
faith, no, not in Israel.

11 And I say unto you, That many shall come from the east
and west, and shall sit down with Abraham, and Isaac, and
Jacob, in the kingdom of heaven.

12 But the children of the kingdom shall be cast out into
outer darkness: there shall be weeping and gnashing of
teeth.

13 And Jesus said unto the centurion, Go thy way; and as
thou hast believed, so be it done unto thee. And his servant
was healed in the selfsame hour.

The first thing I want to point out is that this sickness

was tormenting the centurions' servants. This man was being greatly tortured by Satan. Jesus never turned down anyone who came to Him for healing. He was always willing. Then the centurion said, "Speak the Word only." This is BIG! Speak the Word only! That's why we have to know what God says about our healing so we can speak His Word only. Say what He says, not the doctor or your body or your family.

God has delivered us from the noisome pestilence. No plague shall come near us. You have to believe God's Word in your heart and speak it out of your mouth. If you bought a car and paid cash for it the next thing they would do is send you the title. That's the proof that your debt has been paid in full. Wouldn't you think it was rather crazy if the company called and demanded payments on the car? You wouldn't go for that because you own the title.

Our healing has been paid in full by Jesus. When He said, "It Is finished," it was done. Anything that we would ever need on this earth has been supplied. Healing is in the package. It's inside of the "all things".

2 Peter 2:3

King James Bible

According as his divine power hath given unto us all things that pertain unto life and godliness, through the knowledge of him that hath called us to glory and virtue:

Everything has ears. No, everything doesn't have literal ears like we do as humans, but in a sense it does. God told Moses to speak to the rock. Even though he struck the rock the Bible tells me that the rock responded to his command. You may say, "Well, that was something special God did with Moses." No, it's the same today. That same authority Moses had we have it even greater. We are under a more glorious covenant. Moses had to wait on an instruction from God to move in that type of authority. With Jesus He gave us His name to use at any time. We just have to use it by faith. He gave us legal power of attorney rights to use His power and authority to act on His behalf. This means all born-again believers, the body of Christ, the church, have this right. Do you think Moses would be able to do something that Jesus couldn't do? No! So we can speak to anything that has a name with power and authority. If we believe and do not doubt we can have whatever we say as long as it's in faith.

Philippians 2:9–10

9 Wherefore God also hath highly exalted him, and given him a name which is above every name:

10 That at the name of Jesus every knee should bow, of things in heaven, and things in earth, and things under the earth...

One day, after coming home from work, my ceiling started raining. Water was everywhere. I looked up and realized my bathroom shower was above it and my husband was in it. So I yelled and told him to cut it off. It was leaking. We got a contractor to check it out to see how bad it was and he gave us an estimate of $10,000 or more. No, that was unacceptable. We did not have that kind of money at the time. Our house was already going through a renovation because it was an older home when we purchased it, but that was not in the plan. I had heard of someone speaking to a broken washing machine and it started working again. I knew Moses spoke to a rock. So I said, "Hey, same thing, I can command this pipe to obey."

By this time the workers had cut open the ceiling to diagnose the problem and the pipes were exposed. They would have to redo my shower and some more stuff. It was a big job. So I said, "In the name of Jesus, I command the leak to disappear, seal up and be no more! I resist paying all that money, I won't pay it; you are fixed now!" I told my husband that the problem was fixed and by faith we used our shower that we hadn't used in days. From that day six years ago until today we have not experienced it like that again. However, the leak came back after years of no problems. That's the same as the symptom coming back. Immediately, I said, "No! Leak, you were fixed and you still is now. Dry up!" It did but not all the way. I kept commanding! My husband did go to Lowe's and buy some supplies that were less than $200. I can't remember the exact amount. It was very cheap. He just figured the house being old may need a little TLC. I wasn't having it. I wasn't going to pay a dime. I believe my faith and my husband's wisdom kept us from paying out a five-figure job. Hallelujah! BE IT ACCORDING TO YOUR FAITH.

Experiences and encounters with God will change you forever. The more you know about God and His Son Jesus, the more you grow! We are partners with the Holy Spirit to fulfill God's Word and to enforce His promises.

Talk Back- By now I hope that you have experienced the healing power of God manifest in your body. If this is so, worship God right now. Praise Him lavishly. Pour out your thankfulness.

Not yet, do all the above and add this to it. Talk Back- I know who I am! When Christ died, I died. When He rose, I rose. When He was seated on the right side of the Father, I was seated with Him! As Christ was on Earth so am I. I've overcome Satan! Greater is He that's in me than he that's in the world. IN THE NAME OF JESUS. Sickness, get out of my body NOW! Go! Devil, back up off me, leave now!" Mean what you say and say what you mean. "I am free right now from every spirit oppressing my mind!! Hallelujah! Whom the Son set free is free indeed! I take it, it's mine!"

SN: Closed lips won't get you healed. Talk Back!

Chapter 6

Compassion

When you look at the world, what do you see? The world is filled with so many hurt, broken, and lost people. One of the attributes of our Father is that He is a compassionate God. We have to see people how God sees them. This is the victory! People are blaming God for all kinds of things that the devil is responsible for. How we see Him determines how we trust Him. You cannot say you have faith if you do not trust God.

Many people think compassion means to feel sympathy for someone. It's much deeper than that. Compassion moves you to eliminate suffering. It prompts you to act and relieve that person's pain. You can't rest until you do something about it.

The first thought that comes to mind is, *What if that was me? What if that was my child? How would I respond?* If it was me I would surely want someone to help me. I would want mercy, help, comfort, whatever was needed to eliminate my hardships, suffering and pain. If it were my child I would certainly want the best for them. If it were me I would want the best. A heart of compassion draws near to that person. Usually when there's the death of a loved one, the first thing that I do is give that person a hug. There is usually some type of touch. Their situation must first touch your heart before it can move you to act. The grabbing of a hand or a touch on the shoulder is a physical gesture but compassion takes it further.

The deepest experience I have had with compassion

happened around the summer of 2019. I can't remember the exact date, but I know it was the summer. My client called me because she couldn't make her hair appointment. She wasn't feeling well and she just wanted to rest in bed. I told her it was no problem. I could tell by her voice that it was serious. She went on to tell me that she was bedbound with so much pain. She had kidney stones and the doctors wanted to surgically remove six of them. After she told me, I told her I would be over to her house as soon as I got off. I know I could've prayed over the phone at that moment, but I just wanted to lay hands on her and pray the prayer of faith in person. I had more faith in that than praying over the phone. A couple of hours later, she called back. Up until then I was doing everything I could to get out of there and rush to her because my heart was gripped with compassion. I have never had kidney stones, but I know of someone that I'm close too who has suffered with them on and off for years. I've seen him in pain. He's told me of the hours he's spent trying to get relief. Many stories. I've also experienced the healing power of God's work. Other believers and I prayed for this man and commanded those stones to crush, dissolve, disappear and be gone In the name of Jesus. They did just that. He was healed! (Matthew 18:19).

The second time she called me she said she was in so much pain she couldn't get out of bed and that she needed me to pray over the phone. In my mind all I could think about was that she was too old to be going through that type of pain. She was in her seventies. I couldn't imagine her going through what my other friend went through. I'm told it is equivalent to labor pains without the epidural. That's what I was told the degree of pain felt like. I had to do something about it! My heart was filled with compassion. I prayed a prayer over the phone commanding the stones to disappear out of her body and immediately she started praising God. She responded to each word as it came out of my mouth. Not even after I finished the prayer but as I was praying. She began thanking God; then she said, "The pain is leaving... I feel better... Now it's gone!" All within about a minute. She was out of the bed and she was praising God! She actually came to visit me at my salon because she wanted me to see for myself how the Lord had healed her. Hallelujah! Compassion looks at the whole person—spirit, soul and body. It sees their situation.

This is exactly what Jesus did. He was passing along the road and saw a funeral procession. It was of a young boy. He was his mother's only child. Not only that, but the woman was also a widow. He looked at this woman and was moved with compassion. He went and touched the casket and raised the boy back to life. We can't forget that Jesus was still equally man and equally God. He was just like us. He worked, He had a family and they had real issues. His siblings didn't believe in Him as Messiah. He was rejected, lonely, full of sorrow, misunderstood and lied on. He knows our struggles and can relate. He was tempted from every side and yet He never sinned. He knows what it is to suffer and be mocked and made fun of. Jesus saw the frailty of man and still loved us.

When we see Him, we see the Father. We see the depth of His love, compassion, grace and mercy towards us. It's who He is! He is so very sweet. Our God is a kind, gentle and affectionate God. I find myself telling Him that so much. He's considerate and full of surprises. We get to have a personal one-on-one relationship with Him and experience His glory that abides in us inches away from our mouth resting in our hearts and flowing through our entire being.

That's what I love about the Old Testament. It gives us wisdom and understanding about the nature of God. It displays His heart. It gives us inside information into the graciousness of our Father. It reveals His ways and His mind. The why's and why nots. When I read it, I saw His heart and how He responds, how He thinks, the way He handles the people and also the character of the people. I put myself right in the scriptures with the people and continue to learn from both. I learned from the people and God. There's so much wisdom.

Jesus only did what He saw the Father doing (John 5:19). He was empowered and enabled by the Holy Spirit to have the same compassion that His Father had. We now have the same Holy Spirit. He allows us to see from the eyes of Christ and feel compassion for the world. We are supposed to give everybody what we ourselves have received.

Whenever you are in crisis, hurt, loss, persecuted, and dealing with any type of affliction, know that we have a God who cares for us. He sent Jesus, His only Son, because we were like sheep without a shepherd. We were lost, wounded, sick, orphaned, weak and mistreated with no one to lead us. A real shepherd lays His life down for His sheep. That's exactly what Jesus did for us. He saw the condition we were in. He looked at us with compassion and had to do something about it! These things you have to know about God. Meditate on this knowledge about the Father.

He did not give you cancer or make you sick. He wouldn't take your loved ones away. The church has a poor understanding of who our Father is. Honestly, I get tired and downright indignant sometimes when people say all this bad stuff about my Father. I have to correct them. Like a Father talks to His child He reminds me that it's done out of ignorance. Most haven't been taught right and simply don't have an intimate relationship with Him to know Him in this way. Our victory while on Earth is putting everything in its right perspective. You have to know the whole truth about the finished work of Jesus Christ. Get your mind off your sins. Jesus paid for them all. Past present and future! Get your mind on who you are in Christ. What you focus on the most is what you will become. You will reproduce whatever you focus on! Stay focused on Jesus! Keep your eyes on Him and you will reproduce Him. If you focus on His compassion towards you and mankind that's what you will imitate and produce. Study to see Him right and then receive His mercy, love, compassion, grace in your life. Once you understand what you have it will be easy to give it away. I pray that the Holy Spirit will overwhelm you with His presence and you'll experience Him like you never have before.

Hebrews 4:15

15 For we have not an high priest which cannot be touched with the feeling of our infirmities; but was in all points tempted like as we are, yet without sin.

Matthew 9:36

36 But when he saw the multitudes, he was moved with compassion on them, because they fainted, and were scattered abroad, as sheep having no shepherd.

Lamentations 3:22-23

22 Because of the Lord's great love we are not consumed, for his compassions never fail.

23 They are new every morning;

great is your faithfulness.

Matthew 15:29–39

29 And Jesus departed from thence, and came nigh unto the sea of Galilee; and went up into a mountain, and sat down there.

30 And great multitudes came unto him, having with them those that were lame, blind, dumb, maimed, and many others, and cast them down at Jesus' feet; and he healed them:

31 Insomuch that the multitude wondered, when they saw the dumb to speak, the maimed to be whole, the lame to walk, and the blind to see: and they glorified the God of Israel

32 Then Jesus called his disciples unto him, and said, I have compassion on the multitude, because they continue with me now three days, and have nothing to eat: and I will not send them away fasting, lest they faint in the way.

33 And his disciples say unto him, Whence should we have so much bread in the wilderness, as to fill so great a multitude?

34 And Jesus saith unto them, How many loaves have ye? And they said, Seven, and a few little fishes.

35 And he commanded the multitude to sit down on the ground.

36 And he took the seven loaves and the fishes, and gave thanks, and brake them, and gave to his disciples, and the disciples to the multitude.

37 And they did all eat, and were filled: and they took up of

the broken meat that was left seven baskets full.

38 And they that did eat were four thousand men, beside women and children.

39 And he sent away the multitude, and took ship, and came into the coasts of Magdala.

Jesus saw the condition of the multitude. He was moved to action. He didn't just sit there and feel sorry for them. He met a need and solved a problem which brought relief to the people. Jesus knows all the details of a situation. He reads the heart and mind. He knows the pain that's seen and unseen, spoken and unspoken. His desire is always to do us good not evil. He healed all that came to Him and turned no one away.

Isaiah 30:18

18 Yet the LORD longs to be gracious to you; therefore he will rise up to show you compassion. For the LORD is a God of justice. Blessed are all who wait for him!

Luke 7:11–16

11 And it came to pass the day after that he went into a city called Nain; and many of his disciples went with him, and many people.

12 Now when he came nigh to the gate of the city, behold, there was a dead man carried out, the only son of his mother, and she was a widow: and many people of the city were with her.

13 And when the Lord saw her, he had compassion on her, and said unto her, Weep not.

14 And he came and touched the bier: and they that bare him stood still. And he said, Young man, I say unto thee,

Arise.

15 And he that was dead sat up, and began to speak. And he delivered him to his mother.

16 And there came a fear of all: and they glorified God, saying, That a great prophet is risen up among us; and, That God hath visited his people.

Matthew 20:29–34

29 And as they departed from Jericho, a great multitude followed him.

30 And, behold, two blind men sitting by the wayside, when they heard that Jesus passed by, cried out, saying, Have mercy on us, O Lord, thou son of David.

31 And the multitude rebuked them, because they should hold their peace: but they cried the most, saying, Have mercy on us, O Lord, thou son of David.

32 And Jesus stood still, and called them, and said, What will ye that I shall do unto you?

33 They say unto him, Lord, that our eyes may be opened.

34 So Jesus had compassion on them, and touched their eyes: and immediately their eyes received sight, and they followed him.

15 "Can a mother forget the baby at her breast and have no compassion on the child she has borne? Though she may forget, I will not forget you!

Isaiah 54:10 Though the mountains be shaken

and the hills be removed, yet my unfailing love for you will not be shaken nor my covenant of peace be removed,"says the Lord, who has compassion on you.

Luke 15:4 What man of you, having an hundred sheep, if he lose one of them, doth not leave the ninety and nine in the wilderness, and go after that which is lost, until he finds it?

This is what God has to say about us being His sheep and He our Shepherd:

We are His, He is ours - Psalm 100:3

When we are helpless, He fights for us - Matthew 9:36

We hear His voice and follow it - John 10:27

He knows all His sheep by name - John 10:1–18

Our Shepherd lays His life down for His sheep - John 10:11

His sheep want for nothing - Psalm 23:1

He's our guide; he feeds us, comforts us and leads us to prosperity - John 21:1–25

He's the overseer of our souls - 1Peter-5:4

During my healing journey the Holy Spirit revealed something to me.

He told me that even though we are born again and Satan cannot steal our soul, he is snatching years away from us, killing us before our time. He's stealing TIME. Christians are dying younger and younger from sickness and disease.

I once went to a funeral home to fix the hair of the deceased. As I was putting the final touches on her, a woman came up to me and said that God had just taken her 34-year-old relative with cancer. I had to stop her and tell her the truth. I had to tell her the truth. God did not put cancer on her loved one and definitely didn't call him home at 34. Satan is the root of all diseases. It was loosed upon the earth at the fall of Adam and Eve. We are no longer under that curse now! It's up to us to take authority and enforce our rights. Satan is not going to just leave our bodies alone. By faith we speak the truth over our bodies. 1Peter 2:24 says that by Jesus' stripes we were healed! It's past tense. It's finished work. All we have to do is believe it, speak and command cancer, pain or whatever sickness, or symptoms out of our bodies. Refuse to accept it. Resist it! Look to Jesus and remember the compassion He has toward us. We were healed over 2000 years ago. That means our healing is here now. TAKE IT!

Talk Back! Say, "NO! My Father loves me too much! I know my authority. I know the Word and know that Satan has no right to attack my body with sickness. God in His compassion for me sent His Son to die and every sickness was put on Him so I wouldn't have to be sick. He promised to satisfy me with a long life (Psalm 91:16).

God cannot stand to see us suffer and be sick. He healed the blind, raised the dead, fed thousands because he looked at their situation with compassion and helped them. He did greater for me; He sent His Son to die so I can be healthy, healed and whole! I live in divine health. Every germ, virus and bacteria dies upon contact with my body. Life is continuously flowing to every part of my body. I'm hidden with Christ in God! In order for me to be sick it has to get through God. Thank you, Jesus!Thank you for healing me. Thank you for caring about me!

Matthew 8:17 This was to fulfill what was spoken through the prophet Isaiah:

"He took up our infirmities

and bore our diseases."

Chapter 7

Fear Not

I mentioned earlier in the book that I dealt with fear as a child. There were two things that I believe opened a door for this spirit. The first one is when I was around five years old. My aunt who was about 12 years old at the time made a comment about me having dragon breath. I got up from out of bed with my nightgown on and went into the living room. My aunt was in there, so I ran, jumped into her lap and was all up in her face. She said, “Get your dragon out of my face,” and then pushed me away. I remember that like it was yesterday. From that moment on I thought that something was wrong with me. I didn’t comprehend that simply brushing my teeth like I did every day fixed the problem even if my breath was kicking that morning. I was only five years old or close to that age. I can’t remember my exact age, but I remember the incident. I was always paranoid that my breath smelled and it really hindered my life in many ways. That was the first thing.

Secondly, I did not grow up with my biological dad and was raised by my mom and stepdad. My birth father had two sisters. Both of them died when they were 12. One day, I heard one of my aunts, my mother's sister, say that they wondered if I was going to die young like my aunts. I guess their reason for saying this was because I was the only female grandchild in the family, also because they weren’t saved and had no understanding of the power of their words.

I heard all sorts of things my five-year-old ears

shouldn't have heard. Unfortunately that was one of them. A tiny crack opened with the first incident about my breath. The second one just pushed the door right open to a spirit of fear. That fear of dying early had taken root. When I reached 12 and was still alive, it was a big relief. Next I was wondering if I would make it to 18. I had regular dreams of death. Falling off of a cliff and never reaching the bottom was one of them. It was so scary. I can remember the fear that I felt in those dreams. It was so real. It went from dreams to having visions. I honestly don't know what to call what I was experiencing. I would walk past a person, whether it was a stranger or someone I knew, and instantly see a scene of them dying. They usually were murdered or in a car crash. It always looked like a short movie trailer. It had a lot of action in it, but it was only seconds long.

On top of that I felt like Job in the Bible. The thing I feared most had come upon me. I feared being offensive to people and not getting close to them because I thought my breath was bad. I was so gripped with the fear of experiencing again the rejection that I felt from my aunt. I was in bondage from this almost my entire life. We have to recognize that fear is a demonic spirit. The Bible tells us where it came from. God made sure to let us know it wasn't from Him. Fear is a spirit that comes to torment and create a false belief in the mind. That is what I believe happened to me with the bad breath issue. It was a delusion. Satan made me believe something that wasn't true. Nothing was wrong with me. Fear created a sickness in my body. Do you know that if you think something long enough it will become true? Fear is a magnet and it draws the very thing to you that you are afraid of. That's what happened to me.

The first major issues I had as a child were digestive

issues. I would wake up every morning with cramps and feeling nauseated. My mom took me to the doctor and they couldn't find anything wrong with me. That is a sign of something spiritual and not physical. I did not grow up in a spiritual home where authority could be taken over this spirit. Furthermore, I never told anyone what I was dealing with so I dealt with it in silence.

Fear is a normal emotion put in us by God. It runs the sympathetic nervous system that reacts to fear with a fight, freeze or flight response. Fear prompts a response that is put there to save our life. If I walk upon a poisonous three-foot-long snake, my automatic response is to run for dear life. Yes, fear kicks in, but running for safety is an action that responds to that fear. Not only that but supernatural abilities also kick in. Not only will I run to safety, but I will probably run the fastest I have ever run in my life.

In high school I had my first boyfriend. I definitely wasn't his first or only girlfriend. There was another girl that he dated too and she taunted me every day after lunch. I had never been in a fight with anyone. I was an only child and very sheltered so I didn't have many experiences with confrontation. She picked and harassed me daily. Then I guess she finally decided that she was going to fight me and had a huge crowd follow her this particular day after lunch. It's so crazy because we were even in the same class. I was so scared. I mean really, really scared. She literally told me that she was going to hit me. As she began to pull her earrings off, because of fear of getting hit first, I hit her first. I got strength that I didn't even know I had. I was fighting for my life. It shocked everyone to see how strong I was and how I held my own that day.

I now know that fear releases hormones that increase

and sharpen our functions for survival. We get into survival mode in response to fear. From that day on I never had another problem with that girl. It was as if nothing ever happened. It's just amazing how God so creatively thought of every detail that works harmoniously when He made us. We get supernatural strength and abilities, but there's also another response. Those chemicals can slow down systems in our body too, like our digestive system. Have you ever been so nervous about something that your stomach starts to churn? It rumbles and roars to the point where you have to run to the bathroom. Well, that had happened to me too. The thought of going live on Facebook sent me to the bathroom. I had such a fear of messing up and being in front of possibly millions of people. The fear of being judged or failing and not being good enough sent my digestive system into a rage.

That was the beginning of my health issues that started when I was kid. Many mornings I woke up to nausea and stomach pains. That's because the emotions of a person are connected to the intestines. The gut is a place where sickness begins. Now do you see how all of this came together and why so many people are sick?

God tells us how to drive out that spirit that harasses and torments us. It doesn't come from Him, it comes from Satan. God has given us His Holy Spirit that gives us power, love and a sound mind. (2 Timothy 1:7). The Greek word for power is dunamis. Our English word dynamite came from the word dunamis. We have explosive power in us, power that will totally destroy fear and blast it out of our lives. It's not meant to ever return. Believers have power over that spirit (Luke 10:19). Yes, we have power, but it's not the only thing mentioned in that scripture. It also speaks of love and a sound mind. Let's talk about a sound mind. We cannot expect to have a sound mind without having a renewed mind, a mind that has taken captive all thoughts that don't line up with the Word. We replace the lies of the enemy with the truth of God's Word. We have to know what and how God feels toward us. We have to know all about our newly recreated life in Christ. Our victory over everything that will ever come against us depends on us knowing the truth about God's love for us. That's it. The three have to work together.

1 John 4:18 There is no fear in love; but perfect love casteth out fear: because fear hath torment. He that feareth is not made perfect in love.

Power without knowledge of God's love for us will not work. It is by faith that we use the power, but faith only works through love (Galatians5:6). There are three parties involved in the love equation. We've made mention of two, which is the love between God and the believer. The third one is our neighbor. The Bible makes it clear that we cannot love God unless we love our neighbor. This is true love. So if we don't have love for others then love hasn't been perfected. We really haven't gotten a revelation of God's love for us. We cannot give what we don't have.

1 John 4:20–21KJV

20 If a man say, I love God, and hateth his brother, he is a liar: for he that loveth not his brother whom he hath seen, how can he love God whom he hath not seen?

21 And this commandment have we from him, That he who loveth God love his brother also.

Love never fears because love never fails. Love always wins. It never falls short of success or achievement in something expected, attempted, desired, or approved. So let's say love always causes us to succeed at whatever we attempt, desire and expect. Yes! You will never be deficient or lacking. With love you will persevere and never quit. It keeps you strong and built up. You will never shut down or be crushed by the day-to-day excessive load that living life brings. We will always be able to pay our debts and never be bankrupt. The Bible says love NEVER fails. If you look up fail in the dictionary, put never in front of each definition. That's what love will do for you. That's what I just did above. Love always WINS! It can never fail. If we abide in God, yield and be led by His spirit, our cup will runneth over. How can fear survive where love exists? It can't. Love is too powerful.

God's perfect love casts out fear.

Think of how Jesus drove out the moneychangers with His whip. That's how I see love driving out fear. God says to us that if our earthly parents who are evil know how to give good gifts to their children then how much more will He who is our Heavenly Father give good things to those that ask Him? If He didn't withhold Jesus from us what in the world would make us think He would withhold anything else? He's a good Father who knows how to take care of us, protect us and comfort us. He NEVER would do or give us anything that would cause sickness or harm. He's not the one that makes us sick or causes us to die with it. That's straight from the devil. Satan is the root of it. We can rest in God's love. It's a privilege to call Him ABBA Father.

The first thing Adam and Eve did after they sinned was run and hide from God. They feared punishment. Fear always carries a fear of being punished. What does fear look like? It causes you to run from God and that's what Satan wants. He wants you to feel like God is not enough and that you can't trust Him or take Him at His Word. Fear is a purpose killer. It paralyzes you and isolates you from moving forward and pursuing all the things that God has planned for you. As I'm writing this book we are in the Coronavirus pandemic. I'm seeing the effects of fear right before my eyes. I see the world in crazed hysteria as if they're about to go off the edge. People are fighting and hoarding toilet tissue and simple supplies because of a lack of trust in God. This is the reaction when danger threatens them—the danger of not having enough to survive or not being able to control the outcome of a situation. This spirit's objective is to kill, steal and destroy.

Fear had Elijah suicidal, feeling abandoned and hopeless. The same way faith comes by hearing the Word, which the Bible calls an incorruptible seed. Fear is also a seed. Both come from hearing. Faith comes from hearing the truth and believing it; fear comes from hearing and believing it. Fear is accompanied by lies and Satan is the father of lies. When you hear certain information, that spirit watches to see how you will respond and listens to see what comes out of your mouth.

Our responses have to be of faith. Will you say that God is your refuge, your strength and it's in Him that you trust (Psalm 91:3)? Are you one that repeats every little detail that you hear and read about your situation that doesn't speak truth? It may speak facts, yes, but not truth. It's a fact that the Coronavirus is contagious. But the truth is that thousands may get it all around you, but it will not touch you (Psalms 91:7, 10). Remember what I told you about the importance of words; what you hear, say and listen to will make you or break you.

Words are a seed. This is what happened to Elijah (1 Kings 19). He defended the worship of the God of Israel and had great victory. Then he got a death threat from Jezebel telling him that she was going to kill him like he did her prophets. Elijah got scared and ran. He ended up in the wilderness. He became suicidal and somehow forgot all that God had just done through Him. Jezebel had a bad reputation and was an evil woman, but she was no match for God. Those words were a seed. Elijah let it get into his heart, he believed them and that's how fear came in. What he was experiencing was the fruit from that spirit. He was depressed and wanted to sleep. Satan watches your reaction and through that determines that you're a candidate that he may devour. He pounces on you with one lie after another with an ultimate goal to destroy. When fear is present, problems are magnified. They are nowhere near as bad as it's said and seen. Then Elijah went into isolation inside of a cave. That's exactly what Satan wants, for you to lose your hope and be far from any kind of help from loved ones or those who may be concerned about you. Fear is a tormenting spirit. It's nagging and causes dread. You dread going to work, getting out of bed, eating and even living. It's deadly and dangerous. It will cause you to do things you would never imagine yourself doing.

During this pandemic there were people actually fighting over toilet paper. It's not even an essential that's needed other than what it was designed to do. It doesn't provide any extra security or safety from the virus that's in our nation. People feared not having their needs met. This may not have been the character of any of these people. When fear drives you, it will cause you to react in an unseemly manner. It causes you to embarrass yourself. Fear caused Saul to consult a medium and participate in witchcraft, which was an abomination to God. That evil spirit will drive you to do evil things. It holds you captive, wrapped up in chains, locked up and away from God's best.

I admire the way God lovingly deals with us in our sins. He knows the answer but comes to us with a question. A question opens our mind up to think deeply about a thing. Like He asked Adam and Eve when attempting to hide their nakedness or Jonah when He was angry. Elijah outran Ahab but he couldn't outrun God. While in that cave God asked Elijah what he was doing. In the same way God came to me with a question. I heard a testimony about someone who got beheaded because they would not renounce Jesus as Lord. I thought that was so wonderful. I began to question myself. "Shontesha, are you willing to die for Christ"? As much as I wanted to boastfully say YES, I couldn't. I couldn't with confidence say that I could do it. That was my first time having to face that spirit of fear that had grown up in me. Fear of dying hadn't been dealt with. Then, with a sweet whisper, I heard in my spirit, "Would you die for me?" I wanted to say yes but couldn't. Did this mean that I didn't love Him if I said no? Father already knew the answer. He knew that I loved Him; the problem was I hadn't got a revelation of His love for me. That was a problem. I asked God to deliver me from fear. I couldn't imagine denouncing Christ. That's when Holy Spirit gave me 1 John 4:18.

There is no fear in love; but perfect love casteth out fear: because fear hath torment. He that feareth is not made perfect in love.

First I had to get rid of all the bad doctrine. If you're mixing and trying to live out the old and new covenants you are in bondage and that bondage carries a fear of death with it (Hebrews 2:14–15). God wanted a family with children and relationships, not robots. The main thing is knowing our sins are forgiven, past, present and future. Colossians 2:13–14 (NLT). You were dead because of your sins and because your sinful nature was not yet cut away. Then God made you alive with Christ, for he forgave all our sins. He canceled the record of the charges against us and took it away by nailing it to the cross.

He'll never be mad at you again. Breathe. That's a relief. The worst fear is thinking that God is mad at you and ready to punish you when you do something wrong: No! You have to know that He is your Father and that His love is unconditional. He will never abandon you, lie to you, mistreat you, neglect you or cause any harm to you. He protects and comforts and has great compassion toward you. Fear leaves when we understand this truth. Fear leaves when truth shows up. It's the truth of who God is to you that will set you free.

As I began to write, the Holy Spirit let me know that if He could use those men to write the Bible He can use me to write this book. He told me to make sure every chapter was about relationships with the Father. He wants you to be more in love with Him and for you to understand His love for you. It's easy to get healed when this type of love is experienced. That's how love drives out fear. First we have to have the right knowledge of the new covenant. Then we have to renew our mind with that knowledge, fill it up with all that we learn and know of God's goodness towards us and stay focused there. Then we partner with the Holy Spirit as He leads us and teaches us. As we yield to Him in obedience to God's Word and trust Him with His promptings, we will have encounter after encounter.

One day, while I was at work in my salon, I got a phone call from a man asking if he could come in and get a haircut. I didn't have any openings, but he kept calling and insisting that I do it. By the third time I was getting concerned. It was so strange, unlike anything I had ever experienced. I felt uneasy about the whole encounter. It was dark and I knew it was demonic. I began to stand on the Word of God and say, "No weapon that is formed against me will prosper (Isaiah 54:17) because my faith in God blocks every fiery dot of the enemy." (Ephesians 6:16) He can't do me any harm. NOTHING shall harm me (Luke 10:19). Then I declared confusion over the enemy. That was it! I put my trust in God and left it there.

While I was working in the shop the next day, a man walked in dressed all in white from head to toe with extremely black hair. I had never seen such black hair, even as a stylist. The closest he got was the entrance. He walked a couple of steps through the door and stopped. He began to back up and then he went out the door. I could see him through a mirror I had aligned at my front door. I believe he was the man that had called my shop. He looked confused as he walked in as if he didn't know why he was there. I began to praise God for His divine protection. As I walked to the door I thought of the passage of scripture where Elisha asked God to let his servant see that those (heavenly army) that were with them were greater than the earthly army that was surrounding them. God allowed Him to see a host of angels in chariots of fire that surrounded them ready to bring victory. That day in my shop I was thinking of this passage of scripture as I walked to the door to see if the man was still in the parking lot. What I saw changed my life forever.

When I got to the door and looked out, I saw angels with fiery swords side by side surrounding my shop. God allowed me to see the hosts of angels that protected me. I watched how confused the man was when he walked through those doors. I declared confusion would come upon the enemy and that is exactly what I witnessed. Hallelujah! Not only that, a host of angels surrounded my shop like heavenly bodyguards. They weren't fit to be messed with. No one has been able to change my mind from that day on. I've had people get mad at me because I don't fear the things they do. How can I be afraid after an encounter like that? God loves us that much. We have to just believe God and take Him at His Word and know that He is faithful. He's proved it to me time and time again.

There was another time when I needed money to pay my flood insurance. It was close to $4,000 upfront, no premiums because my shop is by a river. Flood insurance is a federally regulated policy. My insurer told me that federal rates would be the same everywhere. I questioned it because my rates spiked more and more each year. It was just ridiculous. So I talked to God about it. He reminded me that His Kingdom doesn't operate like the world. So I called another insurance company that's local and asked for a quote. He said he would get back to me. The next morning, as I was asleep, I heard a voice telling me to call a friend of mine. I lay back down and went back to sleep because I didn't know if I was dreaming or what. Then it happened two more times. I finally realized it was the Lord. I got up and called my friend around 8:30 a.m. She was up and had come into some money. With two piles on her bed she was deciding if she would send some to me and another person. I'm so glad I listened to the Holy Spirit because she said if I hadn't called she might've changed her mind, but because I did she would send it immediately. I never told her my situation until later. She knew nothing about it. A couple of days after that, I got the check in the mail. That same day a friend walked in and handed me an envelope with money in it she had gotten money from a settlement and wanted to bless me. Hours later, another person walked in and handed me another envelope with money in it and she wanted to bless me from a settlement she had just gotten. I counted all the money and it was only $1600. My flood insurance was close to $4000. I said, "Lord, this isn't enough." It wasn't over yet though. Soon after that, I got a call from the insurance company telling me they had a quote and it was $1563! Hallelujah! God already knew my situation and was waiting for me to trust Him with it. He will send people from the north, south, east and west if necessary. It pleases Him when we put our confidence in Him. I boast mightily on our God. See how He set all of that up just for me. We don't have to fear anything. It is He that I give all the glory to. Who can do all of that but God? He put me on three people's hearts and moved them to action. I laugh when I tell the testimony and say that God even gave me some lunch money with the $37 left over. It is through experience with God. He loves surprises too. Those are the best. There's a reward in putting our confidence in God. He's the reward! We get HIM! I know that He loves me and I believe what He says because of the relationship I have with Him. Knowing God's love for us casts out fear. Love NEVER fails.

I love to read the Book of Psalms and see how David talks about God and His life with Him. He had lived His life with

God as a young shepherd boy killing bears, lions and slaying giants. He knew of God's forgiveness and mercy after He slept with Bathsheba and killed her husband. Many, many times David was rescued by God when He was at the point of death. He knew God personally. The way we live life without fear is to know God. To know the way He thinks and to know His Word. He encourages us 365 times to "Fear Not" one for every day of the year. God doesn't want us stressed out and worried. We can rest in Him because He is with us 24/7. I was reading Psalm 91 I got so stirred up with the fire of God. I mean I was excited praising and worshipping God for His mighty Word. As I was doing this He said to me that this was the old covenant. The one that we have now is even more powerful and glorious. Wow! If His promise of protection and provision was that great then it is even greater now.

Hebrews 8:6But now He has obtained a more excellent ministry, inasmuch as He is also Mediator of a better covenant, which was established on better promises.

Brothers and sisters, be courageous and bold in the Lord. We have a good Father who knows how to care for us in every circumstance. We win! We triumph in all this through Jesus Christ. We are victorious overcomers. Yes, more than conquerors. Pick your shoulders up, warriors. Trust Him. Cast every care upon Him. He can handle it.

Talk Back! Thank you, Jesus, that I am hidden with you in God. I am safe because in order to get to me you have to get through God and that's impossible. I rest in the knowledge of who you are and who I am. I command the spirit of fear to leave now! Go! I will not be afraid because He, the Holy Spirit, is greater in me than he that's in the world. I am bold, courageous and fearless! Lord, you answer me in trouble. You strengthen me when I'm weak. Nothing can separate me from your love. I am yours and you are mine. I shall not live in fear, but I shall live with power, love and a sound mind. There is a reward for putting my confidence in you, Lord. The reward is you. I get you! Hallelujah. Thank you for being my prize. In the name of Jesus. Amen.

Chapter 8

Integrity

Integrity, according to dictionary.com, is defined as: adherence to moral and ethical principles; soundness of moral character; honesty. This is not a one-time act; it's a lifetime commitment to God.

The Holy Spirit had me write this chapter. It wasn't in my plans. I feel like this is the most important one of all. After reading my book and receiving your healing many of you may be the go-to person for healing. You now know who you are and that you have authority over all sickness and disease. Others will be coming to you for prayer to receive their healing. Yes, lay hands on them and command sickness to go in the same way you did with your own body. You have POWER and AUTHORITY over it. As this happens and you get more influence the most important thing to do is remain humble. Keep your heart right with the right motives. Don't get bamboozled with selfish ambitions and pimp the gifts God has given you. Please understand what I'm saying. You don't have to get in a hundred-dollar line in church in order to get prayed for. Make sure you don't use people's weaknesses to take advantage of them. Also you need to be aware of this trap from others. I've seen many tactics where people play on the emotions of people and get them stirred up so they can use them to get what they want. Let the miracles that God does through you and the knowledge you learn be a blessing to others.

Matthew 6:33 says, Seek ye first the kingdom of God and

His righteousness and all these things will be added unto you. This is the key to having favor with God. Your desires should be to imitate God and have zeal to serve people in the same way Jesus did. The more you focus on kingdom business and are not consumed with your own the more God will meet all your needs. There's nothing that you ask for that's in His will that He will hold back from you. This is why you don't have to do anything dishonest. Keep your motives pure and keep your word. Don't make promises you don't keep.

Integrity is truth. It is telling the truth and living our lives as close to God's Word as we possibly can. Character is very important as Christians. This is how we show the world what Jesus is like. It's our witness. The world doesn't need lip-service, they need the gospel. Let them see Christ in you through the life you live. This is the greatest witness for the kingdom. I hear more talk today about religion and the flesh than I do the Good News and the power to live a transformed life in the spirit. Jesus did not die for us to remain the same. He has destroyed the works of the devil (1John 3:8).

We should live a life consistent with biblical morals and principles. I'm not saying we have to be perfect. King David was far from perfect. When he sinned, he didn't try to lie or hide it; he quickly repented. This was a man who struggled in many areas of his life, yet the Bible says he was a man after God's own heart. He didn't have on a mask. The book of Psalms shows us how open and honest David was about his life. He didn't shy away from expressing his true feelings towards his enemies and his own sins. We read about his miseries, victories and failures.

The biggest part of having integrity is being completely

honest with God. He knows it anyway; why not talk it over with our Father? Whenever David reared off, he came back to God in brokenness. When we talk about the kingdom and the lifestyle that we live doesn't match anything that we proclaim, it makes our witness unbelievable. People won't believe you. Inconsistency is the reason why many restaurants don't make it. I say restaurants because of the experiences I've had with new ones. The first few months are great. Of course anything new needs plenty of grace. I really give them a chance. Gradually, the taste of the food changes. The quantity that you get decreases. The service gets poorer. The hours they open and close change until eventually you don't even want it anymore because it's horrible. You don't want to waste your time or money. Once it was the talk of the town, but now is the subject of shame. What happened? Consistency! It's similar to the life of a Christian. Over time it should be getting better and better. There should be some consistency in how we live our lives. We are supposed to make the gospel attractive. We should be drawing, not turning people away. We shouldn't be putting a bad taste in people's mouths. The Bible says, "Taste and see that the Lord is good." Let us be full of flavor. We are the salt of the earth. The way we live our lives should make people want more.

The body of Christ is lacking in discernment. It's falling for everything and cannot recognize the spirit of God from the devil. It saddens me. Do not trade intimacy with God for anything. Seeking and pursuing Him is what He loves. In His presence is fullness of joy. In all of your pursuits let this be number one. It's in this place that your character grows and your heart is purified. There are many benefits to living a life of integrity. I will list five of them from scripture.

1 Psalm 41:12 And as for me, thou upholdest me in mine integrity, and settest me before thy face for ever.

God supports us and backs us up when we keep his ways. It keeps us face-to-face with God. Up close and personal.

2-Proverbs 11:3 The integrity of the upright shall guide them: but the perverseness of transgressors shall destroy them.

Integrity guides you down the right path. Have you ever been confronted with a bribe or asked to lie on your co-worker for a promotion? No matter how sweet the deal, the answer will always be NO. Honesty and love for people will always prevail. Integrity guides your decisions and answers rightly consistently.

3-1 Chronicles 29:17 I know, my God, that you test the heart and are pleased with integrity. All these things I have given willingly and with honest intent. And now I have seen with joy how willingly your people who are here have given to you.

A heart of integrity does good deeds without complaining. It's done willfully and joyfully. Done with the right heart your giving is contagious and causes others to want to do the same.

Proverbs 10:9 You will be safe, if you always do right, but you will get caught, if you are dishonest.

It feels so good to be able to sleep at night. You don't have to worry about being caught. There are no secrets or skeletons in the closet. You have a clear conscience of not having done anyone wrong. Integrity gives you peace of mind.

Proverbs 20:7 The just man walketh in his integrity: his children are blessed after him.

What kind of legacy do you want to leave your children? This tells us that if we really want to bless our children we should live an honest life of biblical moral principles. Live as close to the life of Christ as possible. We don't even hear talk of this kind of thing these days. When was the last time you had a conversation with someone about integrity? The Bible makes it very clear that not only are you blessed but your children are also. The favor of God that is upon your life will definitely flow to your children. Let your life be a testimony and memorial for children and generations to come.

Psalm 112:1–2 (KJV)

112. Blessed is the man that feareth the Lord, that delighteth greatly in his commandments.

2 His seed shall be mighty upon earth: the generation of the upright shall be blessed.

My dear sisters and brothers, look at it like this. You are not trying to become a person of integrity. You were given Jesus' righteousness as a gift. As Jesus was in the earth so are you. So when God looks at you, He sees His Son. It's all about how you see yourself. You don't want to toil. You want to rest. If you saw a dog meowing like a cat you would say to that dog, "Hey, bark like a dog! You're a dog!" You're telling him to bark not because you're trying to get him to become a dog. No, you're telling him to bark because that's what dogs do. It's his identity. Same with us. Now, we're a new creation born of God. A holy priesthood that's righteous. Living life like a fool is like that dog meowing like a cat. That's not who we are. We don't identify with them. I'm not trying to become; it's who I am so I live like it. I fear the Lord, I am honest, trustworthy and of moral character because that's who I am! It's my nature to be like Christ.

Anytime you find yourself acting like a fool,or tempted to be dishonest say to yourself, "NOPE! That's not who I am! As Jesus was so am I."

Proverbs 21:3 To do what is right and just is more acceptable to the LORD than sacrifice.

When you say that you are a person of integrity, that's one thing; when the people boast on your integrity, there's the proof that you are who you say you are. Now, you may have some haters, everyone will. For the most part what do people who know you say about you? Samuel was the man. He lived such a life the people couldn't put their mouth on him to say anything bad.

1 Samuel 12:1-5 American Standard Version (ASV)

12 And Samuel said unto all Israel, Behold, I have hearkened unto your voice in all that ye said unto me, and have made a king over you. 2 And now, behold, the king walketh before you; and I am old and grayheaded; and, behold, my sons are with you: and I have walked before you from my youth unto this day. 3 Here I am: witness against me before Jehovah, and before his anointed: whose ox have I taken? or whose ass have I taken? or whom have I defrauded? whom have I oppressed? or of whose hand have I taken a [a]ransom [b]to blind mine eyes therewith? and I will restore it you. 4 And they said, Thou hast not defrauded us, nor oppressed us, neither hast thou taken aught of any man's hand. 5 And he said unto them, Jehovah is witness against you, and his anointed is witness this day, that ye have not found aught in my hand. And they said, He is witness.

Samuel was a man of Integrity. The people couldn't say anything bad about Samuel. Don't get caught up in the hype. Don't let your head get big. My bishop always tells us leaders to take five minutes and let the air out of our heads. Remain humble because a humble heart can receive grace from God. Be healed, healthy and whole. Refuse to be sick. Don't even believe in getting sick. We don't have to be sick to die. We can just die of old age. As God promised to satisfy you with a long life, leave your family with a legacy of faith in God. Be remembered for your love and faith for the impossible.

Talk Back! Thank you, Jesus, that I am empowered by the Holy Spirit to live an honorable life. I will not look down on others who have not yet received their healing. I will think the best, believe the best and hope the best for others. I speak life and not death. That's who I am. I am Holy. So I live that. I am righteous so I am that. Jesus gave this to me. The old me is gone. I am a new creation. I'm like a stick of dynamite full of power. I have power over sickness and everything that tempts me and tries to harass me. I shall overcome it. I submit to God, resist the enemy and he flees every time. I'm full of wisdom, blessed and highly favored! My children and my children's children are blessed and healthy. They prosper in every area of their lives. We are a power family with moral integrity. We delight in your Word. Great is your name, God! We worship you! In Jesus' name Hallelujah!

Final thoughts

As a child and even as an adult I imagined coming home and seeing my father at the door waiting for me veto come home. When I got there I would run and jump in his arms. Next he would spin me around in the air. It was so much happiness from him as we embraced. This came from me watching movies and seeing this on tv. I knew there were relationships that existed like this but it still didn't seem real. It seemed fake or like a fairytale. I always wanted to experience this in my life. I came from a loving family but there wasn't much hugging or affection. So I longed for this. When I got saved God's love for me has been so lavish and at times left me holding my head. At times even unexplainable. It's because He's not only lovely, He is love. I was debating about whether to add this to my book or not because it felt so silly and childish. I can't begin to count how many times over the years I've sat and imagined this.

While in my living room at the same time my friend called me and told me she was watching a teaching done on the prayer in numbers 6:23-27 called the Aaronic blessing. She said that it had been studied and the image that the prayer gave was as a father kneeling down on one knee and the child running and jumping in the Father's arms with an embrace of love. This was another one that left me holding my head and bursting out in tears. This was nothing but GOD. My friend had no idea what was going on. She knew nothing about what I thought was silliness and right at that moment. All these years what I thought was a childish fantasy, was actually God communicating His love for me over and over again.

It all boils down to knowing and grasping the love that God has for us.

Ephesians 3:17-19 that Christ may dwell in your hearts through faith; that you, being rooted and grounded in love, 18 may be able to comprehend with all the saints what is the width and length and depth and height— 19 to know the love of Christ which passes knowledge; that you may be filled with all the fullness of God.

If you're at home and you get a pain in your body—it could be right now—instead of sitting down and thinking about the pain, believe that Jesus has borne that pain upon Himself on the cross and carried it away. Open up your mouth and command healing now! Not tomorrow, now! If you're healed that means you're not in any pain. Therefore, what would you be doing in that moment if you weren't hurting? Okay, then do it! Get up and get busy doing it 'cause you're healed.

Believe and Receive

Family, the same way we received salvation by faith is the same way we receive healing. When we prayed, we believed by faith that we were saved. Most of us didn't feel anything spectacular. There were no goose bumps or anything like that. We simply had to believe that we got a new heart and new spirit and a miracle happened on the inside of us without feeling or seeing anything. It was invisible. But now you see the results by the transformation of your life. Well, let's do it again. Take your authority and by faith speak to your mountain. Speak to cancer or arthritis. Say, "Cancer, leave my body now! Get out! I curse you. Die and disappear. You will never enter my body again." By faith, believe that it's done. The results of your faith shall manifest now! The moment you believe it has happened. Even if it doesn't feel or look like it, it is done! The same way you got saved you are healed. Now! Not tomorrow. Now. Praise God for it. Look for improvement. It's there. I used cancer as an example. You may be dealing with something else instead of cancer, say whatever it is. Tell it to go and command your body to be healed. Say, "My body responds to

God's Word. By the stripes of Jesus I am healed. It's over! I'm free. Hallelujah!" Praise God, my sister and brother. You're healed and free! Live a life of divine health.

If a lying symptom tries to come back tell it, "NOOOO-

OOO! You cannot come back to my body. Go! I will never accept this sickness, pain, disease ever again." Many times a symptom like gas will try to come back. I do what I just told you. "No! You are a lying symptom! My digestive system is healed." I resist it and immediately it goes away. Don't let anything come back. Our Father loves us. Don't pay for sickness twice. Jesus already suffered for it. You refuse to suffer with it. It was put on Jesus so you won't have to carry it.

I pray blessings over everyone who reads this book. Know who you are and what you got! Family, you got it. Your mouth with God's Word in it is like a sword. It will slice and dice that infirmity right up and out of you. The Word is medicine. Put the Word in your mouth and give it the gos-pill. Do greater works, my sisters and brothers. Open blind eyes; command deaf ears to hear and the lame to walk. You got it. Be free! Turn your city upside down! Be a change agent. It's time for change!

To Book a speaking engagement and receive information about online courses

Contact: Shontesha Price at
shonteshap@gmail.com

If you were healed or have a testimony from reading this book can you please share it by writing a review on amazon.com. Also can you tell others about this book that might need it.

Thank You so much for your purchase!

Andrew Wommack Ministries has 22 years worth of free teachings and other healing resouces on his website www.awmi.net. Check out the healing journeys. It will bless you. His ministry truly has changed my life forever I believe it will change yours too.

www.ingramcontent.com/pod-product-compliance
Lightning Source LLC
LaVergne TN
LVHW021350080426
835508LV00020B/2197
9781735312804